Awakening the Heart

Awakening the Heart

Exploring Poetry
in Elementary and Middle School

GEORGIA HEARD

Foreword by Naomi Shihab Nye

HEINEMANN
Portsmouth, NH

KH

Heinemann
A division of Reed Elsevier Inc.
361 Hanover Street
Portsmouth, NH 03801–3912
http://www.heinemann.com

Offices and agents throughout the world

© 1999 by Georgia Heard

The author and publisher wish to thank those who have generously given permission to reprint borrowed material:

"Like You" by Roque Dalton. From *Poetry Like Bread: Poets of the Political Imagination*, edited by Martin Espada. Copyright © 1994. Published by Curbstone Press. Reprinted by permission of the publisher.

"Red" by Lilian Moore. From *I Feel the Same Way* by Lilian Moore. Copyright © 1967 Lilian Moore. Copyright Renewed 1995 Lilian Moore Reavin. Reprinted by permission of Marian Reiner for the author.

"Quiet" by Myra Cohn Livingston. From *The Malibu and Other Poems* by Myra Cohn Livingston. Copyright © 1972 Myra Cohn Livingston. Reprinted by permission of Marian Reiner.

"My Mouth" by Arnold Adoff. From *Eats* by Arnold Adoff. Copyright © 1979 by Arnold Adoff. By permission of Lothrop, Lee & Shepard Books, a division of William Morrow & Company, Inc.

"Unfolding Bud" by Naoshi Koriyama. Copyright © 1957 The Christian Science Publishing Society. Reprinted with permission from *The Christian Science Monitor*. All rights reserved.

Acknowledgments for borrowed material continue on p. 140.

Library of Congress Cataloging-in-Publication Data
Heard, Georgia.
    Awakening the heart : exploring poetry in elementary and middle
school / Georgia Heard : foreword by Naomi Shihab Nye.
      p. cm.
    Includes bibliographical references.
    ISBN 0-325-00093-X
    1. Poetry—Study and teaching (Elementary)—United States.
    2. Poetry—Study and teaching (Middle school)—United States.
    I. Title.
LB1575.5.U5H43   1998
327.64—dc21   98-29212
                                      CIP

Editor: William Varner
Production: Vicki Kasabian
Cover design: Jenny Jensen Greenleaf
Cover art: Bianca Yeung
Author photo: Eugene Kam
Manufacturing: Louise Richardson

Printed in the United States of America on acid-free paper
05   RRD   14

12/13/05

To Dermot, who has awakened my heart

Work of the eyes is done now
go and do heartwork . . .
Rainer Maria Rilke

Contents

Foreword
Naomi Shihab Nye   xi

Acknowledgments   xiii

Introduction
Poetry, Like Bread, Is for Everyone   xv

One
Making a Poetry Environment:
A Place Where Your Life Really Matters   1

Two
Reading Poetry: Poems Keep Singing to You
All Your Life   18

Three
Writing Poetry: Where Does Poetry Hide?   47

Four
Crafting Poetry: Toolboxes   62

Five
Sharpening Our Outer and Inner Visions:
Poetry Projects   91

Epilogue
Yourself as the Key   117

Appendix A
Guidelines for Revising Your Own Poem, Peer Conferring,
and Response Groups   119

Appendix B
Poets as Teachers   121

Appendix C
Anthology of Student Poetry   123

Appendix D
A Few Good Poetry Books   135

References   137

Foreword

For years now, Georgia Heard has been one of the dearest, deepest champions anywhere in the world for the voices of children. Her energy for the larger life that rises up through reading and writing poetry, her compelling allegiance to experience shaped into language, is a healing tonic for us all. Her words guide us clearly and confidently into our own encounters with young writers because her passion is luminous and true.

I have carried her earlier books, *For the Good of the Earth and Sun: Teaching Poetry* (Heinemann, 1989) and *Writing Toward Home: Tales and Lessons to Find Your Way* (Heinemann, 1995) into countless classrooms around the country. They have befriended me over and over again, and helped me to do better work with students, because Georgia's generosity of spirit and her inspired practical suggestions are so contagious.

In *Awakening the Heart*, Georgia Heard offers useful tools, examples, and stories for teachers and instructors to translate into their own communities—the sorts of things poet William Stafford might have called "portable principles."

How do we create environments in which children will feel safe to make their own poems? How do we present voices we love to young writers in a way that will engage them and invite them to write? What do we focus on? How do we make a fluent translation from reading and talking to writing? How do we tip our heads more curiously and attentively to our immediate lives? What do we draw upon for daily sustenance? Georgia threads the wisdom and discovery of young poets together with the words of beloved well-known poets in a wonderful weave.

Awakening the Heart, a stirring personal reminder that encourages children to discover the words and images of their own lives as we discover our own, is a crucial devotion. We all need such books as lanterns and guides. No matter how long we have been working in similar ways, there will be dim days. There will be clutter and swirling waters and an occasional dip. Our spirits and pencils need tender encouragement to keep breathing.

Awakening the Heart is a book to celebrate and to trust in.

Naomi Shihab Nye

Acknowledgments

Hanging on the wall near my writing desk are the framed words of a French philosopher: "Qui aime . . . forme un circle si parfait qu'il n'y a aucun terme a l'amour," which loosely means "Whoever loves . . . forms a circle of love so perfect there is no term to describe love." I've been reading these words now for more than fifteen years. There are so many people who have helped form a perfect circle of love for me and who have helped make this book possible.

For the past fifteen years, I've returned to my home away from home in Arizona to work in Phoenix area schools. I'd like to thank Carol Christine of the Center for Establishing Dialogue, and the many dedicated teachers and educators who have made a profound difference in my own life and in so many children's lives: Kitty Kazcmarek, Kathy Mason, Mary Glover, Nancy Grubb, Dick Thomas, and Sue Sutter.

I'd also like to thank Lucy Calkins and the Teachers College Writing Project. Several years ago Lucy invited me to participate in a Leadership grant to lead a two-year study of poetry with an exceptional group of teachers. It is from these monthly meetings, long weekend retreats, and work in their classrooms that many of the ideas in this book came to fruition. I'd particularly like to thank Grace Chough, Andi Kramer, Cathy Grimes, Cathy Kelly, Rory Freed, Norma Chevere, Michele Caputo, Susan Levy, and Isaac Brooks.

I'm also grateful to the Hawaii School District teachers and educators and to the teachers and students at the Iolani, Kamehameha, Punahou, and Epiphany schools. My work has been blessed by their graciousness, dedication, and poetic sensibility. Thank you to Karen Ernst and her colleagues at Kings Highway Elementary in Westport, Connecticut, who have changed my thinking about the role of art and writing in the classroom.

I'd also like to thank Francine Ballin, principal of the Greenacres Elementary School in Scarsdale, New York, and all the wonderful teachers and students there; my friend James Sullivan, now the Scarsdale writing consultant; and the Edgewood Elementary School.

Rachel Schulman, Susan Pomerantz, and the other dedicated teachers and administrators who work with exceptional children (who have an innate sense of poetry) at the Herbert G. Birch Services School have been an inspiration to me.

Many thanks also to Irene Tully, Deb Foster, Karen McKee, and Nancy Remkus for their friendship and for feeding me brilliant poetry ideas; Bev Gallagher, poetry lover extraordinaire, and to the other teachers and students at the Princeton Day School in Princeton, New Jersey; the poetry-loving staff and teachers in the Clayton, Missouri, School District; the Mary Institute and St. Louis Country Day School and, in particular, Michael Gerard and Kathleen Armstrong; my dear friend Ellin Keene at the Public Education and Business Coalition in Denver, Colorado; the inspiring company of faculty and students at the Northeastern University Martha's Vineyard summer workshops; and finally, Susan Van Blarcom and the talented staff and students at the Crofton House School in Vancouver, BC.

I also wish to thank the people at Heinemann: Karen Hiller, my speaking agent, whom I've met only once but whose voice has become so familiar these past five years she seems part of my family; Susie Stroud and Cherie Lebel of Heinemann Workshops; Vicki Kasabian, who shepherded the book through production with great skill and care; and Bill Varner, fellow poet and wonderful editor.

And finally I'd like to thank Dermot O'Brien, my husband, who when I return home tired but inspired from traveling always completes my perfect circle of love.

Introduction
POETRY, LIKE BREAD, IS FOR EVERYONE

After I gave a poetry workshop for teachers in Denver, I returned to my hotel room and through the thin walls I heard a woman say to her husband, "I went to a poetry workshop today . . ." I immediately grabbed a glass, tiptoed up to the wall, placed my ear against it, and listened. "The woman giving the workshop said that everyone has poetry inside of them." She paused. "Do you think I have poetry inside me?" Her husband said, "I don't know. Maybe." It took a lot of self-control for me not to yell, "Yes!" as if a voice from beyond. Then she said, "Who knows? Maybe someday I'll find it."

We all have poetry inside of us, and I believe that poetry is for everyone, but can we recognize it when we hear it, in our students and in ourselves? Sometimes it disguises itself, it doesn't rhyme, it doesn't sound like a limerick, so we have to look for it in unlikely places. M. L. Rosenthal said, "There is so much poetry present in the voices of people to whom it would hardly occur that this could be so. The way we all speak in unselfconscious moments is the very stuff of poetry." The way we speak to our loved ones every day and night: when you tuck your children into bed; the first thing you say to your spouse or partner when you wake up in the morning. When we speak in a voice that's exclusively ours, that's natural, when we're not trying to be anything other than ourselves, that's the stuff of poetry.

But many of our experiences of poetry began in school. They were not always positive. The experience of reading a poem to find the "hidden meanings" was often frustrating and destroyed the pleasure of reading poetry. As a result, many of us feel about poetry as Jean Little describes in her poem "After English Class": "It's grown so complicated now that, . . . / I don't think I'll bother to stop." Many teachers have told me stories of their unpleasant first experiences. A third-grade teacher once told me, "When I was in high school my teacher gave me a C on the first poem I ever wrote. I thought my poem was really good—but what did I know? I thought 'she's the teacher she must know better,' and never attempted to write another poem again."

Another teacher explained, "I had to memorize part of 'The Rime of the Ancient Mariner' and recite it to the whole class. I was so shy I had a stomachache weeks before. No wonder I dread teaching poetry now."

I have heard a few positive experiences of poetry but, unfortunately, they are the exception rather than the rule—stories of fathers, mothers, grandmothers, grandfathers, and teachers who infused a true love of poetry into people's lives. The predominant memories are negative or, like my own, nonexistent.

Now I'm beginning to understand the answer to Adrienne Rich's question "What is it that allows many people in the United States to accept the view of poetry as a luxury rather than food for all: food for the heart and senses, food of memory and hope?" Perhaps it's the way it has been taught and presented to us that makes so many people exclude it from their lives.

During the past ten years since I wrote my first book, *For the Good of the Earth and Sun*, I have seen the transformational power of poetry—the power to feed the heart and senses. I've experienced it in my own life, and I've seen it in schools in almost every state in the United States— from farm schools in Iowa to the classrooms of New York City. I've crouched next to a six-year-old girl who closed her eyes and sang her sweet poem to me: "The sky is an angel's pool. / God is their lifeguard." I've hugged a fourth-grade boy who was in tears as he wrote a poem about how his father had been killed by drug dealers. I've listened to young teenage kids, just released from prison, read their poems about their sad lives, and I saw how thirsty they were to tell the "stories of their souls." I've sat beside a kindergarten boy who looked out at his fellow six-year-old poets and read, "There is only/One insect/One bird/One tree and/One Planet." After a moment of silence, he said, "Think about it." And we promised that we would.

The kids I have taught have helped me see that the real lessons poetry teaches are much larger than counting five-seven-five on our fingers, or thinking of the best rhyming word for *moon*. The real lessons poetry can teach are what I call life lessons. They are the foundation of *Awakening the Heart*. Each chapter, from setting up a poetry environment to teaching craft, reflects these life lessons.

One of the most important life lessons that writing and reading poetry can teach our students is to help them reach into their well of feelings— their emotional lives—like no other form of writing can. Howard Gardner says that math and verbal intelligences are seen in most schools as the most important of the eight intelligences he identifies. But among the other intelligences are knowing and managing one's feelings (intrapersonal), and understanding and getting along with others (interpersonal). Gardner argues that an education that ignores these two important intelligences is incomplete. The very nature of poetry can teach our students this kind of emotional literacy.

My hope in writing *Awakening the Heart* is to return the heart to the teaching of poetry, and to help us all realize that poetry, like bread, is for all of us—as Roque Dalton describes in his poem "Like You":

> Like you I
> love love, life, the sweet smell
> of things, the sky-blue
> landscape of January days.
>
> And my blood boils up
> and I laugh through eyes
> that have known the buds of tears.
>
> I believe the world is beautiful
> and that poetry, like bread, is for everyone.
>
> And that my veins don't end in me
> but in the unanimous blood
> of those who struggle for life,
> love,
> little things,

> landscape and bread,
> the poetry of everyone.
> *(translated by Jack Hirschman)*

It can also help our students open their eyes to the beauty of the earth, restore a belief in the power of language, and help them begin to understand the truths inside them.

1

Making a Poetry Environment:
A Place Where Your Life
Really Matters

When I moved back to New York City two years ago I brought my writing desk with me. It's really not a desk at all but a harvest table I bought at a secondhand store in New England. I tied it to the top of my Subaru station wagon one summer and drove from Maine to New York.

Whenever I think of a harvest table I think of the table on the screened porch off the kitchen at my grandparents' house in New Hampshire when I was a girl. It was called a harvest table because throughout the summer vegetables harvested from a neighbor's farm covered the top—string beans, corn, and in late summer, zucchini and yellow squash. My sisters, cousins, and I sat at the table sorting and snapping string beans, shucking corn, and cutting yellow squash into penny pieces as we talked. I'm sure I bought the table, paint cracked and peeling, to remind me of those long, abundant summer New Hampshire days.

On my harvest table in New York, I can almost see the silky strands of corn silk from our shucking but instead of vegetables there are drafts of poems, a wooden box of pens, a poem by Lucille Clifton, and an eagle feather given to me recently by one of my students. The table faces three large bay windows and, best of all, my precious maple tree—one of the reasons I can continue to live in New York City. The tree's branches and leaves touch the windows so in the summer I feel like I live not in an apartment in the city but in a treehouse. The tree is filled with subtle stories of the delicate

1

spring buds opening cautiously in April, the last leaves clinging to the tree through December, and the small birds protected by leaves from a summer thunderstorm. These stories, and others, are part of my daily sustenance.

In my apartment, I also seek out other ways to remind me of the mysteries and miracles of the world. On the wall next to my writing table I have hung, among other things, a postcard of the million-year-old cave paintings in France, a picture of Georgia O'Keeffe in her eighties alone in her studio, a photograph of a Hopi boy, a picture of Mt. Chocorua (the mountain I spent childhood summers gazing at), a piece of driftwood I found at the beach the day my grandmother died, and a photograph of a rocking chair on a porch to help me remember to slow down and feel. I don't necessarily write poems about these objects, but I surround myself with them, because they bring to mind the places and people I have met who have changed my life in some way. I paste quotes on the walls of my apartment:

> "The perfectionist writes with one eye on her audience. Instead of enjoying the process, the perfectionist is constantly grading the results."
> "Creativity is not and has never been sensible."
> "Shoot for the moon. Even if you miss it you will land among the stars."

And Einstein's wise words:

> "Imagination is more important than knowledge."

The objects and photographs are reminders that I need to lead my life as a curious and passionate human to keep my heart open, and to create an environment where I'm nurtured as a poet.

When someone deeply listens to you

It's not the desk or the objects around my apartment that are important but the feelings they evoke. It's the emotional environment that matters in making a poetry environment. Similarly, the emotional climate of a classroom is one of the most important factors in setting up an environment that will nurture the poet inside all of our students. Richard Hugo wrote: "When we are told in dozens of ways that our lives don't matter . . . a . . . [poetry] workshop may be one of the last places you can go where your life still matters."

A classroom environment can send out messages: that all of our students' lives matter; that every voice is worth listening to; and that students can take risks in writing poems about whatever their hearts urge them to write. I focus on creating the emotional environment first, and then I trust that the poems will follow. Here are a few things to keep in mind.

1. We must learn to listen deeply to our own images, thoughts, and feelings—and to our students'. John Fox describes this kind of deep listening in his poem, "When Someone Deeply Listens to You." He says when we are truly listened to "a beloved land that seemed distant is now at home within you." We need to help our students find their images and voices—their "poetry homes."

2. Every student needs to know that the classroom is a safe place where every voice is respected. Writing poetry is about learning to express our deepest feelings and experiences through words, and that can be very frightening. Alice Walker describes the power of poetry for kids: "Poetry breaks through the skin of suffering in which children are often imprisoned: silent, confused, scared. A child's poetry is an intimate, trusting gift to her parent or to anyone who wishes to 'read' her heart." A respectful and safe environment can ease these fears and inhibitions and help students write more honest poetry.

3. Poetry is already present in the classroom before we formally introduce it. Listen to your students talk, and find the seeds of poems in their natural, everyday voices. This, of course, doesn't mean that we're listening for words that rhyme but words that feel true, expressions that surprise or describe something in a new or beautiful way. I collect these overheard lines of poems in a notebook, then read them to the class. Or make a class poem—a kind of "found poem"—from the collected poetry seeds.

Irene Tully, a colleague and friend, posted a sign on her classroom bulletin board at the beginning of the year that read What We Say Is Poetry. She listened for her first graders' spoken poems and stopped them if she heard a poem trying to be born. One day she and her class went for a walk outside. When they returned to the classroom to talk about what they had noticed Jacob said, "The clouds were opening and the sun was closing and the grass was turning back and forth." Irene thanked Jacob for saying such a beautiful poem, and asked if he would write it down so they could honor his words by displaying it on the bulletin board under the What We Say Is Poetry sign. Another student, Mariel, saw an in memoriam plaque on a pear tree in the school's front yard and said, "I saw the sign of the deadness on the tree." And Michael, while gazing at a piece of coral in a jar of water, said, "It looks like flowers blooming in the water."

As their "caught" poems began to fill the board, students listened for the poetry in each other as well. Kids are amazed that what they say every day is poetry, and when we point it out to them they become aware of the beauty and the poetry in their own voices.

4. I didn't know until I was in high school that poets were actually alive and currently writing poems. Include your students in the larger world of poetry and poets. Read them what poets say about poetry, the process of writing poems, and living life as a poet. Show them photographs of poets so they know what poets look like, compare your students' poems to professional poems, show them Bill Moyers' and David Grubin's *The Language of Life* and *The Power of the Word* videos of poets reading and being interviewed. Refer to your students as poets. This connection with the poetry world outside the classroom will help your students feel that they're part of a larger community—that poets are real—and are listened to and respected in the world.

5. Truly believe that every one of your students has the potential to be a poet—especially the struggling ones. Often their urgency to express their feelings, stories, and souls helps them write the most powerful and truthful poems. Cynthia Rylant observed this when she told the story of meeting a boy whom she knew was a poet:

> I once met a boy who read *Waiting to Waltz* and he said to me, "I know just what you mean . . ." And he proceeded to describe to me what it was about the Western Auto Store that hit him the way a good sunset hits you and I thought to myself, This boy's a poet. I believe he was born with that way of looking at things. . . . and even if he never writes one single line of poetry, he'll always be a poet. And the people around him will mutter about how intense he can get sometimes, and his teachers will complain about how he never pays attention and people will wonder why he can't just lighten up . . . What they don't understand is that he's seeing all those small meaningful things they're missing . . . but this boy, he's the real poet, because when he tries to put on paper what he's seen with his heart, he will believe deep down there are no good words for it, no words can do it, and at that moment he will have begun to write poetry.

6. Celebrate each student's unique way of looking at the world. Poems reside in this innocent vision. Once in a kindergarten class in New York City, a boy walked up to me and said, "Excuse me," as he pulled on my skirt. I crouched down next to him. He had a little bowl haircut and huge brown serious eyes, and I knew that whatever he wanted to tell me was very important.

"Do you know what I want to be when I grow up?"

"What?" I said.

"A dinosaur skin finder."

"What a fascinating job!" I said, curious about his new future profession, "What would you do? What would your job be like?"

"I'll go around the world and find all the dinosaur skins then take them to the museums and stretch them around the bones." I thought, just like in the Museum of Natural History in New York, where at the entrance is a true-to-life replica of a dinosaur.

I could have, at that moment, informed him that, in fact, his job was impossible—that he'll never be able to find any dinosaur skins because they don't exist and therefore, he better think of another job. But it wasn't the job that was important—in time he'll learn about how museum dinosaurs are made—it was his innocent vision of the world that was so refreshing—and where poetry is sparked.

7. We shouldn't wait until May or June to begin exploring poetry when all the "important things" are completed. To make time for poetry, we have to believe that reading and writing poetry will give our students more than a good score on a writing test.

A living poetry museum

Max Van Manan wrote: "When we enter a classroom, we soon have a sense of what pedagogy is practiced there. . . . A classroom speaks of the ways children come to know their world." In many classrooms I've visited, teachers have created places filled with trust, respect, and deep listening as well as the fascinations of the world and the seeds of poems, where I want to sit down and write.

The poet Patricia Hubbell created an environment when she was a girl that nurtured poetry for her:

When I was ten years old, I started a museum in the playhouse in our backyard. I filled the shelves with birds' nests, rocks, shells, pressed wildflowers, and other treasures. I spent long hours in the woods and fields collecting things. I took long walks and kept my eyes eagerly open.

One day, I found a snakeskin, complete from head to tail. The thin papery skin was beautiful. I put it on a shelf where the sun would shine through it.

About the time I started the museum, I began to write poems. I wrote about the sun and the rain, about riding my pony, about swimming in the ocean. I wrote about the things in my museum. Birds' nest and rocks, leaves and butterflies found their way into the poems.

Fran Rosen, a second-grade teacher in New York, created a classroom environment that reminded me of Patricia Hubbell's living museum. Right away, I saw that it was a place where poetry could easily be written. When I asked Fran how she was able to create such an abundant environment, she said, "I think of making my room like my grandmother's attic—filled with treasures yet to be discovered."

In her room, she had a fish tank with poems about fish pasted all around it and clipboards nearby that students could use to write their fish observation poems on. In a corner was a chart where kids could write down any questions they had about their lives, the world, anything they were curious about. She placed examples of question poems in a basket that kids read for inspiration. She framed part of a window with crepe paper and called it the "poetry window"—where kids could look out, daydream, observe the world, and write down what they saw. She pinned a map of the world on the wall, surrounded by poems about different places, poems about traveling, poems in Spanish and other languages. Students were invited to locate the states and countries their families were from, find poems or songs about these places or about traveling, and pin these to the map.

There was a table with milkweed pods, shells, and birds' nests on it—beloved objects the kids had brought in—where kids could go to sniff and touch the objects, and be scientist-poets and write down what they observed. Fran set up a small table with a tape recorder and headphones where kids listened to their favorite poems on tape, and made their own tapes of favorites. In the back of the room she brought in a small picnic table where kids sat and read poems by Langston Hughes,

Lilian Moore, and other poets, then watercolored or drew the images they saw in their minds.

Fran had sewn six pockets onto an apron, filled the pockets with her favorite poems, then hung the "poetry apron" on the wall. Kids were invited to take a poem out of the pocket and add it to their poetry anthologies, but they had to replace it with a poem they liked. Finally, there was a bulletin board with newspaper clippings of current events on one side; on the other side kids were invited to pin poems they wrote or found about the world issues that concerned them.

Poetry study centers

After visiting Fran's classroom I was inspired to devise what I now call "poetry study centers"—ten areas where kids can independently explore poetry. Each center is designed as a hands-on study area for kids, kindergarten through high school, to explore one aspect of poetry. Creating poetry centers in the classroom expands the possibilities of poetry, helps kids know that poetry can be playful and inspiring, and shows them that they can take charge of their own learning. Each one of these centers can be presented to the whole class, or set up for small groups of three to five kids. Poetry centers can be used in any way the teacher thinks best. The following are some suggestions:

- Fran's classroom was larger than most but you don't necessarily need a lot of space to set up poetry centers—students may bring center materials back to their desks to work.
- It's overwhelming to have all ten centers going at once—five or six centers at one time is more manageable.
- The format of poetry center time is similar to a writing workshop: begin with a brief minilesson to discuss either the content or management of the poetry centers; follow with center time, which is usually about twenty to thirty minutes; and end with a sharing time.
- I walk around the room and confer with my students as they work in centers just as I would during the writing workshop.
- Sometimes it's helpful to introduce each center to the whole class first, so kids are more prepared to work in small groups.
- Students can stay in one center for one day, several days, or a week, and then rotate to the next center.
- There is no particular order to setting up these centers.

The following is a description of the ten poetry centers, including materials teachers will need to set them up and directions for students.

AMAZING LANGUAGE CENTER

The purpose of this center is to foster an awareness, an appreciation, and a love of words—both their meaning and their sound. It's also a place where students will learn that poetry can be found almost anywhere—not just in poetry books. A bulletin board labeled Amazing Words could be the beginning of this center—a place where students post amazing, beautiful, interesting, vivid words and sentences collected from stories, poems, and spoken words heard around the classroom. When I introduce this center, I first define what I mean by "poetic." I tell students to listen for words that make a picture in their mind; are an unusual or surprising way of expressing something; give a strong feeling; or evoke a memory. There are many ways to create word awareness—here are four:

Treasure Hunt for Poetry Gather several books that you've already read aloud to your students or that they're familiar with, not necessarily poetry books. Poetic picture books, such as Cynthia Rylant's *Night in the Country*, Jane Yolen's *Owl Moon*, or Ralph Fletcher's *Twilight Comes Twice*, or a nonfiction book such as Jean Craighead George's *One Day in the Alpine Tundra* is often a good choice for the language center. Have a chart ready or cut bookmark-size oaktag for students to write down their collected words and lines.

Directions to Students:
Sit with a partner and treasure hunt for poetic lines or words in these picture and nonfiction books you've already read. Write them down on a piece of paper. Next, choose one line from your selection, write and illustrate it on a bookmark—be sure to include the title and author of the book.

From Cynthia Rylant's *Night in the Country* kids in a third-grade class discovered these poetic lines: "Great owls with marble eyes who swoop among the trees. . . Night frogs who sing songs for you every night. . . ." Ralph Fletcher's picture book *Twilight Comes Twice* is one long poem:

With invisible arms
dawn erases the stars
from the blackboard of night.

And much of the writing in Jean Craighead George's nonfiction book *One Day in the Alpine Tundra* sounds like a poem: "In this mysterious light a breeze dropped a fragment of lichen on the scar left by the fallen slab of rock. It sent out a root in the melt of a hailstone. The healing began."

One class donated their "poetry treasure bookmarks" to the school library for other students to take when they checked out library books.

Cracking-Open Words An important part of writing poetry is being able to "crack-open" overused and abstract words and sentences such as: "It was a nice day" or "She was very nice" and find the image inside. In this center, students can experiment with an important part of revision—cracking-open words, phrases, and sentences to find more accurate and vivid images inside. (See Chapter 4 for examples and exercises.)

On a large piece of paper write several generic sentences and place an equal sign next to each one. Writing with images takes practice—as seen here in this fifth grader's first and second attempt at cracking-open the sentence:

It was a nice day. = "It was exciting and the snow was beautiful."

It was a nice day. = "The snow was falling like feathers from a big bed."

His first attempt at finding the image was just as abstract as the original, and we still can't see the picture he sees in his mind. But in his second attempt he paints a vivid picture.

Directions for Students:
None of the sentences below give us a picture in our minds using words. Next to each sentence describe and write what you see in your own mind.

Word Scramble One of the values of the Magnetic Poetry Kit (magnetized words for the refrigerator to create poems from) is in helping poets experiment with using words that we might not choose on our own, and expanding our vocabulary so we can surprise ourselves with unusual combinations of words. Instead of buying a Magnetic Poetry Kit, students can make their own "word scramble kit" for the class.

Gather sentence strips for students to write words on, and scissors to cut out the interesting words they find. You can categorize the word search into parts of speech. Ask each group to look for words in a particular category, write them on the sentence strips (use a different color for each category of words), and cut them out. Ask your students to choose words that relate to their lives in some way. Here are some examples of words kids have thought of:

Noun	Verb	Adjective	Colors
tree	jump	clear	blue
water	buy	shiny	red
sound	sing	soft	black
family	hear	sharp	
bird	break	light	

Small Words	Endings	Prepositions	Pronouns
the	s	below	he
and	ed	above	she
it	ing	beyond	we

Directions for Students Making the Word Scramble Center:
On a large piece of paper write a list of interesting words—words that have to do with your life, what you know, or what you see every day. Now write the words on sentence strips and cut them out. The other poets in the class will eventually use these words to create poems.

Directions for Students Making Poems:
Lay the words out on a table or on the floor so you can see all the words at the same time. Create a poem or several poems using just these words.

Here is an example of a poem the kids created from the words above:

The black
     bird   sings
clear
sharp
                    beyond
the   breaking
               water.

Finding Word Sound Personalities Words have different personalities and qualities according to their sounds. Poets write by considering the meaning and the sounds of the words. Make a chart, writing these three words and leaving space underneath for lists of words: smooth, bumpy, and sharp (see page 90).

Directions for Students:

Think about the sounds of words. Find at least three words that sound smooth, bumpy, and sharp. For example, a word that sounds smooth is ice; a bumpy word is hippopotamus because it has many small syllables that make your mouth move; and a sharp word is kite because the consonants are sharp.

LISTENING CENTER

Listening to the sounds of a poem is like laying a welcome mat in front of the door of poetry. Poetry is meant to be heard, and listening to a poem adds a new dimension to our experience of it. To set up this center, you'll need a tape player and a few headphones. Either make a tape recording of your favorite poems or buy recordings of poets reading their poems. Later, invite kids to make recordings of their favorites.

Directions for Students Listening to Poems:

Listen to the poems on this tape. As you listen, choose a favorite line, image, or poem and when the tape is finished illustrate the images you saw in your mind.

Directions for Students Making Their Own Tape:

Choose a favorite poem from your own personal poetry anthology, and practice reading it out loud. Then record your poem on the tape. Make sure to pause at the end of lines, and read slowly. Suggestions for reading poems out loud:

- *Read the poem very slowly. Linger over each word without sounding unnatural.*
- *Pause slightly after every line and in between stanza breaks.*
- *Emphasize words or parts of the poem that feel important.*
- *Put yourself behind the words of the poem—show your listeners that you really care about the poem you are reading.*

DISCOVERY CENTER

Poets are like scientists, and many poems are sparked by observations. The discovery center uses this important tool to fuse science and poetry. In this center, students become close observers of the small, ordinary, and fascinating objects in nature and in the world around us.

Bring in some interesting objects from nature, such as a nest, shells, or interesting plants, and also invite kids to bring in things from the outside world. Place these items on a shelf or a table to make a discovery center. Find poems, or ask your students to find poems, that have observation as their source, and display them around the center as examples. You can place an observation journal on the table for your students to record what they notice, or they can write in their notebooks.

Directions for Students:

Choose one of the natural objects from the table. Take it to your desk and make several sketches. As you're sketching, write down the details you're noticing as well as any other thoughts—what it looks like or reminds you of—or questions you have. After you're finished observing, try to create a poem from your notes. Read examples of observation poems in the basket for inspiration. Or divide a piece of the paper into four boxes. Using the following headings, describe the object you've chosen:

Describe what it looks like.   Describe what it feels like.

Compare it to something else.   Do you have any questions?

POETRY WINDOW AND OBSERVATION CENTER

Outline part of the classroom window—to be used as the "poetry window"—with crepe paper or some other material. Display observation poems about the outside world—sky, trees, the parking lot, cars—around the window or in a basket as examples. Have clipboards and paper at the window ready for students to write their observations. Some kindergarten and first-grade teachers have placed an easel by the window with large paper and a marker attached with a string. Students paint the images they see using words or pictures.

Directions for Students:

Look out the window and write a list of five things that you see outside. Now choose the most interesting thing from your list, and de-

scribe it. Write a poem using your description. You can read the other poems in the basket or around the window for inspiration.

ILLUSTRATION CENTER

Many poems contain images—words that give us pictures in our minds. The purpose of this center is to help kids become aware of these internal mind pictures. Select three or four poems that contain images, and place them in folders. Have blank white paper, colored markers and pencils, and watercolors available for the kids to illustrate with.

Directions for Students:

Choose a poem from the folder. Does the poem create a picture or pictures in your mind? Illustrate the image you see, or, if you see several images divide the poem up and create a picture book. Either you can create your own picture book or each person in your group can illustrate one page of a group picture book.

PERFORMANCE CENTER

This center makes poetry come alive by performance. You can include simple props such as paper-plate masks and fabric for kids to use when they're performing poems. Kids can choral read, act out, dance, or sign a poem. One first-grade class performed a poem using silent movements, and the rest of the class guessed which poem they were performing.

Directions for Students:

Choose one of the poems in this basket. You can dance the poem, choral read it, or act it out. Practice your performance for the rest of the class.

MUSIC CENTER

Music and poetry are two threads from the same cloth. A music teacher in Scarsdale, New York, Trudy Moses, gave me the ideas for this center. Select a favorite poem and write it on a large piece of paper. Gather a few musical instruments such as a triangle or a small drum.

Directions for Students:

Read the poem on the chart and explore how the word sounds (long, short, smooth, bumpy). Add some movement to the words (this will usually center around the verbs). Find an instrument whose sound expresses or matches the word or words you've chosen. For example, for the words "sparkling stars" choose an instrument that sounds "sparkly" to accompany the words. Read the poem, playing the instruments with the selected words. Then read the poem again, and don't speak the selected words, only play them.

REVISION CENTER

In this center students will have the opportunity to experiment with revisions such as rearranging line-breaks, cutting out excess words, and condensing a poem. Select a poem and rewrite it as a paragraph.

Directions for Students:
Read the poem on the chart. I've added and changed endings on words, changed the line-breaks, and made it look and sound like a paragraph in a story. Revise the poem as if it were your own—cut out extra words or endings and rearrange the line-breaks. Make two revised versions, and then look at the original.

An example of a poem I've used is "Red" by Lilian Moore:

(Story version)
I was standing at my window and all day I saw across the way, on someone's windowsill, a geranium which looked like it was glowing red bright—it looked like a tiny traffic light faraway.

(Original version)

> **Red**
> All day
> across the way
> on someone's sill
> a geranium glows
> red bright
> like a
> tiny
> faraway
> traffic light.

POETRY EDITORIAL CENTER

Poetry can be sparked not only by nature and memories from our personal lives, but also by what's happening in the world around us. In preparation for this center, ask the kids to bring in newspaper clippings or written thoughts about events and ideas they're concerned about in the world. After discussing the articles and concerns, post them on the News Bulletin Board and leave space for poems.

Directions for Students:

Reread some of the newspaper articles that we've collected and discussed. Choose one of the articles that interests you and write down any feelings, questions, or thoughts you have. Create a poem from these reflections to display as an editorial.

POETRY READING CENTER

Collect a variety of poetry books in a basket or bin. Choose books that the kids know as well as books that they might not know or select on their own. You can create a basket of books by one poet, or books about a certain theme like nature or deep feelings. Create a comfortable and cozy place with pillows, a rocking chair, or couch, and a lamp. Place a card at the back of the books for kids to write comments and recommendations to their fellow poets on.

Directions for Students:

Choose a poetry book, make yourself comfortable, and read. If you love a certain word, line, or poem you can write it in your notebook and save it for later. At the back of the book, write any comments you may have about the book or a particular poem to share with the other poets in the class who might choose this same book.

In classrooms where centers have been created the environment is humming with possibility and abundance, and I am inspired at the depth and beauty of the children's poems that were just waiting to be spoken or written.

Creating a poets' room

One morning in Norma Chevere's sixth-grade class in East Harlem, New York, she and the poets in her class discussed what poets need to surround themselves with to affirm and inspire their work. They discussed what poets' desks looked like—not clean or cleared of every object but stacked with drafts of poems, inspiring books, photos, quotes, and sometimes natural objects. Norma asked her students to bring in what they needed to surround themselves with as poets. Her students brought in treasures throughout the year and placed them on their desks.

When I visited Norma's classroom, I saw thirty-five poets working diligently at their desks. But these were not the usual bare desks that I see in most classrooms. These desks looked liked my harvest table—covered with quotes, photographs, books, and other objects of inspiration. I wanted to sit down with them and write. As I walked around the room, I saw:

- Each one of Norma's students kept a writer's notebook decorated with photographs, quotes, and poems.
- Some writers had special pens because they said they could only write in a certain color ink; others chose to write with pencils.
- They placed quotes, poems, and favorite lines in frames on their desks or laminated them on the surface.
- Each desk had on it a favorite book, or stacks of books, that the student had just read or was inspired by.
- Self-portrait poems (see Chapter 2) hung off the front of their desks.
- Framed photographs of families, friends, and pets sat on top of their desks.
- Almost every desk had a natural object on it for inspiration such as a feather, beach glass, or a small stone.
- Several poets kept drafts and revisions of poems in folders on their desks.
- A few kids had stuffed animals propped on their desks as souvenirs of their childhood.

They didn't write poems about these objects—the artifacts were there to nurture their creativity. The four walls of their classroom also reflected a thriving writers' community:

- Poems by student and adult poets, words explaining their process of writing poetry, and poems illustrated by students were put on large posters and hung on the walls.
- Each student had watercolored and written about one place where they found poetry in their lives, and these were strung along the ceiling on a clothesline.

- Four or five favorite poems displayed in Plexiglas frames hung around the room—to make a "poetry art gallery."
- There was a rug in the back of the room near an extensive collection of poetry books, with big pillows for sitting on and leaning against and a poet's chair for sharing time.
- There was a bulletin board to honor unusual, surprising, or beautiful words collected from student poems, books they were reading, and overheard conversations.
- They had set up a mentor's shelf—a separate shelf in the classroom library devoted to poets who inspired students' writing.
- Reproductions of famous paintings found in the Metropolitan Museum of Art hung among the poems on the walls to integrate the process of painting with the process of writing.
- The class chose a poem together and displayed it above the classroom door. Each morning they recited it together before poetry workshop.

But ultimately, it was not the objects that made Fran's and Norma's rooms special, nor was it the poetry window, nor the photographs on the kids' desks—these things were there just as a reminder to open our eyes to the things of this world and to the richness of our inner lives.

2
Reading Poetry: Poems Keep Singing to You All Your Life

As a child I remember walking outside with my mother one cold, windy November day when she recited a poem I've heard dozens of times since:

> The north wind doth blow
> And we shall have snow,
> And what will poor robin do then, poor thing?
> He'll sit in a barn,
> And keep himself warm,
> And hide his head under his wing, poor thing!

My relationship to poetry began there. I pictured a raggedy little robin out in a barn alone shivering, and I couldn't do anything to help it because it was inside my imagination—inside the poem. I still find myself reciting that poem in November when a cold wind begins to blow. I also still sing, when I see one star in the sky, "Star light / star bright / first star I see tonight . . ." and make a wish. Or if I'm having a bad day I'll concentrate on avoiding the cracks in the New York City sidewalks for fear of breaking my mother's back—or however the poem goes.

The poems I heard when I was young weren't always deep, but the relationship I formed with them was. They seem like gifts to me, for when I heard them I had no idea they were poems. It wasn't until much later that

I went to libraries and bookstores and discovered poets like Rainer Maria Rilke, Lucille Clifton, Seamus Heaney, and Langston Hughes and learned that reading poems could help me understand my life.

Sometimes I love whole poems and write them down in my notebook but often I just save parts of poems. Years ago, during a difficult time, I cherished these wise words from Stanley Kunitz's poem "The Testing Tree":

> . . . the heart breaks and breaks
> and lives by breaking.
> It is necessary to go
> through dark and deeper dark
> and not to turn.

More recently I've carried Whitman's advice with me:

This Is What You Shall Do
Love the earth and sun and animals
Reexamine all you have been told,
At school, at church or in any book,
Dismiss whatever insults your own soul
And your very flesh shall be a great poem.

The Lithuanian Nobel Prize–winning poet, Czelaw Milosz, reminds us in his poem "Ars Poetica?" that when we read poetry "our house is open, there are no keys in the doors, / and invisible guests come in and out at will."

One of the reasons to invite poetry into our lives and into the lives of our students is to meet our invisible guests—grief, joy, anger, doubt, and confusion. We read poetry from this deep hunger to know ourselves and the world.

I learned several years ago what a lifeline poetry could be when my ninety-nine-year-old grandmother died. It was a rainy soft October morning when I heard the news. It meant that both my grandparents who had lived at Oldfields were gone, and that chapter of my life had come to a close.

This was the grandmother who, ten years earlier, when I told her I wanted to be a poet, said that she would help pay my way through college if I became a cartographer instead. Stubborn as I was, I said no. Several times before she died, she told me how sorry she was for not believing in me, but she was afraid that I wouldn't be able to make a living. She also told me how proud she was.

On the day she died a friend made me an anthology of poems about life and death as a gift. The anthology helped me. As Donald Hall writes, "Poetry enacts our losses so that we can share the notion that we all lose—and hold each other's hands." It began with an excerpt from "After Apple-Picking," a poem by Robert Frost, that I had read many times before—but in this context the poem changed because my grandmother's death had changed me: "My long two-pointed ladder's sticking through a tree / Toward heaven still . . ."

The next page of the anthology contained the final lines of the "The Long Boat" by Stanley Kunitz:

> As if it didn't matter
> which way was home;
> as if he didn't know
> he loved the earth so much
> he wanted to stay forever.

The final "poem" in the anthology was a poetic passage from *Charlotte's Web*:

> Wilbur never forgot Charlotte. Although he loved her children and
> grandchildren dearly, none of the new spiders ever quite took her
> place in his heart.

These poems gave me comfort. They became companions and my solace during this time of grief. I carried the anthology around with me like an old friend.

Kids need to become friends with poetry as well. They need to know that poems can comfort them, make them laugh, help them remember, nurture them to know and understand themselves more completely. As one poet said, "There is something about poems that is like loving children: they keep returning home and singing to you all your life."

How do we ensure that poetry has a chance to sing to our students? How can we help our students form a relationship to poetry? How can we guide them toward poems that will include their varied lives and stories— poems that will speak to their hearts? We can do this by understanding the layers of reading poetry.

The traditional way of introducing poetry is to begin by interpreting and analyzing a poem—dissecting its meaning and structure—which is meant to give insights into the heart of the poem. Unfortunately, it never does. Instead, it only alienates many people from the world of poetry.

There are three layers to uncover when reading poetry. And each layer, if considered, will help ensure that poems will sing to our students and that they'll seek out poems even after the study of poetry has ended in the classroom.

The three layers of reading poetry

1. Choose poems to read that are immediately accessible, nonthreatening, and relevant to students' lives—encourage reading projects that will invite all students into the world of poetry.

2. Help students connect personally to a poem by guiding them toward finding themselves and their lives inside a poem.

3. Guide students toward analyzing the craft of a poem, figuring out how a poem is built, interpreting what a poem means, or unlocking the puzzle of a difficult poem.

Layer One: Choose poems to read that are immediately accessible, nonthreatening, and relevant to students' lives—encourage reading projects that will invite all students into the world of poetry.

We need to ensure that every one of our students has a positive and successful experience with poetry. In order to guarantee this, we should pick poems that speak directly and simply to them, and not begin with reading the most difficult poems. This does not mean that we must necessarily begin with Shel Silverstein or with other light verse; rather, select poems that show a range of emotions and a variety of subjects so students get a sense of poetry's possibilities. Poetry needs to begin to feel as natural and fun to our students as holding a pencil or writing their names.

THE LIVING ANTHOLOGY PROJECT

One of my favorite poems is on the walls inside the Broadway 104 bus next to the advertisements for podiatrists and divorce lawyers. It's a poem by Nina Cassian entitled "Please Give This Seat to an Elderly or Disabled

Person." At first I thought it was a sign at the front of the bus reminding passengers that the front seats are reserved for the elderly, but on second look I realized it was a poem. This poem and others on the buses and subways in New York City are the work of the Poetry in Motion Project whose goal is to bring poetry into the ordinary and everyday experiences of our lives. I watch people on the subways and buses after they've settled into their seats look up and read a poem, look away, then look up and reread. Who wouldn't rather read a poem than read every detail of the ads for podiatrists and Swatch watches? If only one or two people each day are inspired from these poems to buy a poetry book, the fate of poetry is changed.

Adrienne Rich wrote, "A series of poems by a lot of poets has been up in the New York subway . . . and I think it should be happening everywhere. I think the question of 'how do we get people to read poetry?' might be to some extent resolved if people saw more poetry in just the ordinary public places where everybody has to stand on line . . ." Thanks to the Poetry in Motion Project and similar projects, poetry is no longer silently tucked away in the backs of bookstores or buried on the least popular shelves of libraries. It's accessible to more and more people, and for this reason is enjoying a resurgence.

When I was a member of the Columbia University's Teachers College Writing Project the secretary, who was also a poet, had an idea similar to the Poetry in Motion Project—to post poems in public places. She chose the one-room women's rest room to display a different poem weekly. Her poetry selection was quite varied and included many contemporary poets such as Mary Oliver, Adrienne Rich, and Molly Peacock. Apparently, the poems were so well liked that they began to disappear. So she added a note above each poem: "If you like this poem please don't take it off the wall! Come to 331 Horace Mann and get a copy." Women from all over the college stopped by to request copies. One day an older man walked shyly into the office and asked her for a copy of one of the poems. A little suspicious, the secretary asked, "What were you doing in the women's rest room?"

He said, "I'm the window washer, and each time I clean the windows I look forward to reading the poem in the bathroom. And this one reminds me of my daughter—I'd like to send her a copy."

The idea was simple and it gave hundreds of different women (and at least one man) a chance to stop and read a poem. After all, it does seem that the rest room is the only place that we have a chance to rest during the day. Why not accompany it with a poem?

Years later, when I returned to Teachers College to give a workshop, I noticed that the women's rest room had been renovated. Instead of one room, there were three stalls. I was disappointed because I thought that that was the end of the poetry idea. When I walked into the first stall I was surprised; several of Mary Oliver's poems were posted on the wall, as well as a short bio and photograph of her. Each stall had been transformed into a poet's study! And, as before, I saw the familiar sign: "If you would like a copy of this poem . . . ."

This idea of placing poems in ordinary and familiar places gave me the inspiration for a project I call the Living Anthology Project. Poetry anthologies often sit quietly on the shelves in libraries, but a "living anthology" is a collection of poems that come alive on the walls of the classroom, school, town, subway, or streets so that poetry can become a familiar and everyday presence in people's lives.

I first launched the Living Anthology Project at the wonderful Princeton Day School where I had been invited to come as a visiting poet. In my first meeting, with Bev Gallagher's third-grade students, we all sat on the floor. Some sat cross-legged, some were lying down, and a few boys gathered in the back, perhaps still a little wary of poetry.

I began, "You know one of the things that I've been thinking about lately is how you just don't see a lot of poetry around. And I was asking myself How can we make sure that poetry is all around us so people can have the opportunity to read it? I thought that today we would begin a project together. I call it the Living Anthology Project. Instead of collecting poems we love and putting them in a book, we'll make an anthology out of the walls and spaces around the school. It will be our jobs to make sure poetry is all around the building so other students and teachers can have a chance to read some poetry. In a few minutes, we'll take a tour of the building to search for good places to put poems. To start with, we'll look for a place where people wait in line with nothing to do, a place where they could just as well read a poem that's right there on the wall. For example, we could place a poem by the water fountain or in the cafeteria or when people first enter the school. So grab your clipboards, pencils, and paper and we'll begin the tour."

With clipboards in hand we set on a scavenger hunt of the building searching for places where we could pepper the school with poems. As we walked along, the kids couldn't contain their excitement. Some were frantically scribbling down places, others were pointing and saying things out loud like:

"How about here on the wall next to the water fountain?"

"Or here on the cafeteria walls so while kids are waiting in line to get their food they can read a poem?"

"Or how about on the bottom of the trays?"

The other kids were writing these ideas and more down on their clipboards:

"How about here going up the stairs?"

"In the front hall so you can read it when you first walk in to the school."

"In the school office so people can read a poem while they wait."

They were overflowing with ideas.

After the tour we returned to the classroom to share. Bev wrote their ideas on a large piece of chart paper. The list was overwhelming, covering the entire chart. So we decided to look over the list and begin by selecting four or five places. It was difficult to choose but finally the four places the kids decided on were: by the water fountain, on the cafeteria walls, by the front entrance to the school, and at the checkout counter in the library. We would save the other ideas for later.

In many classrooms where I've introduced the Living Anthology Project, I've brought a bag of poetry books from the library, but Bev's classroom was filled with more poetry books than in many school libraries. She is a true lover of poetry, and her extensive poetry collection reflects the importance she gives poetry throughout the year. Bev pointed to the books on the shelves and said, "Remember when you find a poem you think will match one of the four spots, just put a Post-it Note to mark the place and write which place you would recommend putting the poem. In a half hour we'll come back to the rug and share."

I added, "Remember, be creative in your choice. If you're choosing a poem for the water fountain you can pick a poem about water but you can also be imaginative and pick a poem about thirst, or waiting in line, or anything that has to do with that area." Some other suggestions Bev and I offered were:

• Read the poem over carefully. You can choose part of the poem or the entire poem.
• Think about all the different ages and kinds of kids who will be reading these poems—choose poems for kindergartners as well as for older kids.

- Ask yourselves: Do you think the poem will grab your fellow students and make them want to read more?
- Choose a poem that will surprise.
- Find poems that speak about your experiences of, for example, checking out books in the library or standing in the cafeteria line.
- Look for poems that will help people look at their surroundings in a new way.
- Choose poems that will compel people to stop and take a little time out of their busy day to enjoy a poem.
- Be sure to include the poet's name and the title of the poem or book—in case anyone wants to find the book in the library or a bookstore.
- Write your own poems to display.

And so kids crawled under desks, went to the far corners of the classroom, and began to read. As I walked around, I noticed that every child was reading intently, some in pairs, others in threes or fours, and some alone. That day the kids chose so many poems that Bev decided to make folders to store them to use later on.

After they selected the poems, we talked about the best ways to display them. Should they all be displayed in the same way like the Poetry in Motion poems on subways and buses? Or should some be written on large posters? Others in small Plexiglas frames? Or should each place chosen dictate how the poem looks? How about illustrating the poems? Should there be more than one poem in one place at a time? How often should the poems be changed? Should we elect a rotating group of Living Anthology assistants to be responsible for displaying the poems? What about placing an envelope with copies of the poems inside for people to take? After discussing and deciding these issues, they went to work. Here are two poems that the students chose:

For the library—displayed in a Plexiglas frame on the counter near where kids check out books:

Quiet
Myra Cohn Livingston

QUIET

it says
in the library

QUIET

and what I want to know is

what's quiet
inside the books
with all those
ideas and words

SHOUTING?

For the cafeteria walls:

My Mouth

Arnold Adoff

stays shut
  but
food just
finds
  a way

           my tongue says
we are
  full today
  but
        teeth just
            grin

and
say
      come in

i am always hungry

Since that time in Bev's class, I've introduced the Living Anthology Project to many different grades and schools. In a marvelous school in St. Louis, I even found Robert Frost's "The Gum-Gatherer" underneath a student's desk next to a wad of gum! In addition to creating a poetry-friendly environment in the school, one of the purposes of this project is that it helps kids read many different kinds of poetry books in a non-threatening atmosphere where there's no right or wrong answer, or test to be completed. Now kids are contributing to the growing popularity and accessibility of poetry so that more and more people can discover that, contrary to what they expected, poems can be an integral part of every-day life.

Dancing, acting out, or choral reading a poem helps students "climb inside a poem" and make the images and the words of a poem come alive. In the introduction to the anthology *Poetry Out Loud*, Robert Ruben writes:

> Certain poems come alive when read out loud. They may wait quietly on the printed page, dressed neatly in rhymes and stanzas, sheltering modestly beneath clever titles. But when read aloud they explode with life and color and fervor. Poetry was a way of speaking before it was a way of writing: it was language arranged memorably, given pattern and form so it would not vanish into empty air—so it could be passed along.

That should be our goal, to help poetry come alive with life, color, and fervor. When I'm choosing poems I look for poems with:

- two or three different voices built into the poem
- a pattern
- a refrain
- a definite rhythm or beat
- vivid images
- a story.

The class can choral read a poem in a variety of ways:

- The whole class reads the poem together.
- The teacher reads a few lines, then the kids repeat the lines.
- Divide the class into two groups—one group reads a few lines, followed by the second group reading a few lines.
- Snap your fingers or clap your hands to the rhythm of the poem—be sure to listen for places where the rhythm changes.
- Read the poem out loud as a class and whisper a few words or lines of the poem.
- Read the poem in a round.
- Read the poem in a natural voice, and then choose one word or line to read in a louder or softer voice.

- Three quarters of the class reads the whole poem and one half of the class repeats one significant word or line of the poem continuously.
- Sing the poem—make up your own tune or use a melody from a song you already know.
- Kids stand in different areas of the classroom and read lines from there.

For acting out poems I suggest:

- Turn the poem into a play—write a script for it. Illustrate the images or the story of the poem first and then decide how to act it out.
- Act out the literal meaning of the poem or the deeper symbolic meaning.
- Express the feeling or the personality of the poem through drama.
- If the poem connects to students' own lives act that connection out.
- Students use silent movements to act out the poem and ask the rest of the class to guess which poem it is.
- Learn sign language and sign the poem.
- Use simple props to help the performance come alive.
- Apply movement to a few key lines or words of the poem.
- Dance the poem.

POETRY RITUALS

Poetry has always been chanted and read ceremonially as a way to honor or commemorate an event or person, open and close the day, or mark a significant transition such as a birthday or graduation. That's why over a billion of us flock to gift stores to buy cards with mostly mediocre poems on them written by people employed by Hallmark or other gift card companies. Even if someone has never read a poetry book, most of us have bought poetry on a birthday or get-well card and know that poetry is special enough to give as a gift.

In Ralph Peterson's wonderful book *Life in a Crowded Place* he writes about the value of rituals and celebrations to mark the transitions and events of our lives. One important transition that happens every school day occurs in the morning when kids leave the world of home and enter the world of school. He encourages teachers to acknowledge this important transition, as well as others, with meaningful rituals. Reading poetry is a natural choice for these rituals.

Native cultures have chanted and sung poetry to mark significant times and events for hundreds and hundreds of years: the Navajo people—as part of their Blessingway ceremony—sing a series of dawn songs and poems celebrating that delicate time when night turns to morning; in Africa, many tribes sing songs and poems to usher in the day. In fact, one picture book for children entitled *I Am Eyes* begins with a translated Swahili phrase celebrating morning:

> The sun wakes me.
> I say,
> "Ni macho!"
> It means, "I am awake."
> But it says,
> "I am eyes!"
> I see sunflowers and skies.
> I see grasses and giraffes.

The book continues with a list of what else a person might see when he or she first wakes. Kids can chant this poem, and add their own litany of what they see when they first wake.

Many schools honor the beginning of the day with announcements and the pledge of allegiance. Karen Makee, a first-grade teacher, invited her children to write their own beginning of the day pledge. They wrote it as a poem. It's called *Our Pledge:*

> I wish the world was clean.
> I will try to make it that way.
> I wish there were no more wars,
>   that people would be nicer to each other.
> I wish there were no more guns. No more violence.
> I'm glad we have homes.
> I will try and help those who don't.
> I'm glad we have the world.

The poem hangs on a banner in the class. They recite it as a group or choral read it every morning to begin their day, and kids are encouraged to add on to the poem whenever they feel they have something new to pledge.

There are many other events and transitions that poetry can help celebrate during the school day. We can read poetry to celebrate the beginning of every season, every month, birthdays, and each new moon (we can name the moons like the Navajos and other Native Americans do). We can:

- Give poems as a gift to a student on his or her birthday—or mark any special occasion with a poem.
- Place a poem that the class chose together on the door of your classroom—begin each day reading that poem.
- Make one day a week a special Celebrate Poetry Day—kids can recite poems they've chosen to memorize, perform poetry, or spend time in poetry centers.

You can invite poetry naturally into the classroom by making your own poetry rituals that will help poetry sing to your students. Keeping a record of the daily poem on a chart or calendar will help kids remember poems they've heard over a period of time. There doesn't necessarily have to be any deep discussion or interpretation of the poem—if we simply allow our students to savor a poem's words and feel what it has to say to them each day, that's the beginning of inviting poetry to sing to our students.

The very nature of poetry is that it is a moment away from the every day ticking of the clock—a little epiphany. We invite poetry into our classrooms and our lives to stop the quick pace, to slow us down, to help us to take a little moment away from "business as usual," to reflect, to feel, and to celebrate.

A POEM AS UNFOLDING BUD

Reading the same poem more than once models the process of reading poetry—because a poem is more condensed than a story and its meanings are sometimes hidden. Naoshi Koriyama describes this process in this poem "Unfolding Bud":

> One is amazed
> By a water-lily bud
> Unfolding.
> With each passing day
> Taking on a richer color,
> And new dimensions.
>
> One is not amazed,
> At first glance
> By a poem,
> Which is as tight-closed
> As a tiny bud.

Yet one is surprised
To see the poem
Gradually, unfolding,
Revealing its rich inner self
As one reads it
Again
And over again.

The class might choose a poem like Langston Hughes' "My People" to read every day for one week.

My People
The night is beautiful,
So the faces of my people.

The stars are beautiful,
So the eyes of my people.

Beautiful, also, is the sun.
Beautiful, also, are the souls of my people.

The format for the week might look like this:

Monday: Read Langston Hughes' poem "My People" out loud to the class. Read it twice—sometimes poems are over too quickly, and it's often difficult to digest a poem after one reading. Invite your students to close their eyes and, as you read, ask them a few questions—not necessarily about the meaning of the poem but about their personal response to it. For example, What does the poem make you feel? Listen to the sounds and meaning of the words—what stands out for you? Does the poem remind you of anything in your own life? What pictures do you see in your mind? Then afterward, anyone can share briefly with the whole group. Asking too many questions might make the discussion seem like a quiz where there's a right and wrong answer. The most important thing I keep in mind when I read a poem is to make sure there's a lot of silence around this first reading.

Tuesday: Read "My People" again. Ask your students to draw or paint a picture of the images the poem paints in their minds. They can illustrate the poem on a single sheet of paper, or they can divide the poem's lines and illustrate on separate sheets and make a picture book. Another way to illustrate a poem is to make a personal collage—cutting out pictures from magazines and copying personal photographs and including those in the collage. When students share their illustrations, each one will be different because each person will have his or her own interpretation of the poem.

Wednesday: Read "My People" together as a class. Ask the students to express each line of the poem through arm and hand movements. For example, when I've introduced the "signing" of this poem to students this is what they've come up with:

My People	**Interpretative Movements**
The night is beautiful,	*Arms above heads, open wide as if to embrace the whole night sky.*
So the faces of my people.	*Fingers touching faces.*
The stars are beautiful,	*Arms above heads with fingers opening and closing—like the sparkling of the stars.*
So the eyes of my people.	*Fingers resting delicately on the corners of eyes.*
Beautiful, also, is the sun.	*Arms in front, rounded, open wide and then, moving up like the rising sun.*
Beautiful, also, are the souls of my people.	*Hands on chests to show the soul, and then moving away from the body to show how the soul goes out into the world.* This line can be expressed in many different ways depending on what people believe about the soul. In Hawaii, the native Hawaiian students and teachers placed their hands below the stomach at "the gut" because they believe that the soul resides there.

Another way of using interpretative movements to express a poem is to ask students to form small groups and transform "My People" into a play, then act it out.

Thursday: Ask your students to bring in a personal response or connection to "My People": a letter, a photograph, an object, another poem, a book, a song, or anything that will help them connect to the poem. The poem becomes like a stone thrown in the pond—the connections and responses are like circles emanating out from the center, growing larger and encompassing more of the pond—more of your students' lives.

In one class, kids brought in family pictures—one girl brought in a photograph of our planet because she said, "All of us on this planet are my people," another student brought in a letter from her Mexican grandmother, and one boy brought in an article about homeless people because he said, "People forget that we have to take care of people with no homes because they're our people too." Everyone's response to "My People" was different, which adds to the beauty, understanding, and universality of Langston Hughes' poem.

Friday: Have a final group reading of the poem. Those who have chosen to memorize the poem can recite it to the class. Ask if anyone wants to include a copy of "My People" in their poetry folders.

There are many ways to guide our students to interact with a poem—depending on the type poem, of course. Here are some other ways:

- For several weeks, read excerpts from Langston Hughes' biography, as well as more poems by him. Discuss how the circumstances, beliefs, and events of his own life and the world around him are reflected in his poems. Make a list of the kinds of things you know about Langston Hughes' poetry: What does he write about? How would you describe the voice in his poems? What is the feeling or the mood of the poems? How does he use line-breaks, rhyme, image, pattern?
- Ask your students to underline a line or a part of "My People" that feels especially true or memorable to them, and ask them to explain why.
- Write a real or imaginary letter to the poet telling or asking him anything they'd like to know.
- Write a call-and-response poem. For every one of Langston Hughes' lines, write one of your own in response—like a poem for two voices.

My People	**My People Response**
The night is beautiful,	*The night is wise,*
So the faces of my people.	*So the words of my people.*

The stars are beautiful,
So the eyes of my people.

Beautiful, also, is the sun.
Beautiful, also, are the
    souls of my people.

The stars are infinite,
Our eyes are the windows of
history.

Beautiful.
My people. My people.

We want our students to connect to poems personally first, and then we can dig through the layers of meaning and find all the "hidden meanings"—the rhyme scheme, the form—with excitement and joy as our guide.

Layer Two: Help students connect personally to a poem by guiding them toward finding themselves and their lives inside a poem.

We can help our students form their own relationship to poetry by giving them poems that will touch their lives in a personal and meaningful way.

POEM AS GIFTS

One second-grade teacher gave a poem as a gift to each of her twenty students—one poem a week. She searched for a poem each week that would acknowledge, encourage, and affirm a particular student. There was one boy who was having difficulty making friends, and she took a risk and gave him this poem by Myra Cohn Livingston:

Finding a Way

I'd like you for a friend.
I'd like to find a way.
Of asking you to be my friend.
I don't know what to say.
What would you like to hear?
What is it I can do?
There has to be some word, some look
connecting me to you.

He seemed a little more comfortable in class after that.

After a few weeks the kids began to send poems to each other as well. They began to exchange poems back and forth like baseball cards. They were beginning to make friends with poetry. And beginning to recognize their lives in poems.

POEMS ON DESKS

One middle school teacher told me how she began her poetry study by tap-ing poems on her eighth graders' desks. When they entered the classroom she told them not to sit down right away but to walk around, read the po-ems, and try to sit at a desk that had a poem that they liked or that reminded them of their lives taped on it. After searching for a while all her students sat down, and they began their poetry study by reading the poems out loud and sharing why they chose to sit at that desk with that particular poem.

SELF-PORTRAIT ANTHOLOGY

What we ultimately want from a poem is what Beverly McLoughland suggests in her poem "Surprise":

> The biggest
> Surprise
> On the library shelf
> Is when you suddenly
> Find yourself
> Inside a book—
> *(The hidden you)*
>
> You wonder how
> The author knew.

After my grandmother's death, I carried around my "life and death anthol-ogy" everywhere I went. It seemed I had never connected to poetry so deeply before. I had never depended on poetry to help me get through the day, never thought poetry was about my survival. I began to ask myself, Have any of my students ever felt this way about poetry? How can I help them experience poetry in a deeply personal way—not necessarily just over grief, but over joy, frustration, and love? I wanted my students to find themselves and their lives buried in a poem and, finally, I thought of a way that I could do this. I call it a Self-Portrait Anthology. As Charles Simic says, "A poem is someone else's snapshot in which you see yourself."

I introduced the self-portrait anthology in a fifth-grade classroom in Arizona. It was a double class of forty kids, so the environment was not particularly conducive to intimacy. We all sat on the floor together. Many of the students had a kind of quiet shyness, perhaps thinking Who is this stranger sitting on the floor with us? A group of girls sat together in the very back of the class against desks looking like they were expected to be bored.

After telling them a little about myself, I told the story of my grandmother's death and read them my anthology. I explained that I wanted them to connect to poetry this deeply and personally. I said, "When Van Gogh painted one of his self-portraits he painted his face green. Although obviously he was not really green, he was expressing some inner feeling about himself. I want you to search for one self-portrait poem that expresses your inner feelings. It's a little different from other anthologies where if you like cats, let's say, you find a poem about a cat. This type of anthology has more to do with who you are inside. Are you a shy person? Or a person who makes other people laugh? What's your personality like? What's been on your mind lately? This first poem that you find today is going to be just the beginning of your self-portrait anthology—eventually it will be a collection of poems that will show many different parts of yourself."

Rather than presenting them with a tower of unknown poetry books, I took a quick tour through the poetry books that I had gathered from the library to give them a head start in thinking of which book they might choose. I held up a few of Myra Cohn Livingston's series of books—*Poems About Mothers, Poems About Fathers, Poems About Brothers and Sisters*—and asked, "Does anyone have a special or difficult relationship with anyone in your family, and think you might find a self-portrait poem in here?" A few kids waved their hands eagerly. And I handed the books to them.

"Is anyone here an animal lover and think you might find a self-portrait poem in this book *Turtle in July* by Marilyn Singer?" Two students waved their hands, and took the book to read together. "Any sports fans? Here's Arnold Adoff's *Sports Pages*. Or Jane Yolen's *Bird Watch* for bird lovers. If anyone is going through a difficult time—a divorce or any trouble at home—this book, *There Was a Place and Other Poems*, also by Myra Cohn Livingston, might be for you."

By the end of the tour most kids had a book in their hands, and only a few wanted to keep looking through the remainder of the poetry books. Several books were so popular that kids formed reading groups and read the poems out loud together.

I also gave them small Post-it Notes to mark the place of a few poems, and then to select one to share with the class that day. Once they chose their poem, I asked them to copy it into their notebooks and then write the reason they chose it beneath the poem.

On that first day I had no idea what to expect. Two girls were sitting with their backs against the wall, their knees up, quietly chanting the words of the poems from Walter Dean Myers' *Brown Angels.* As I walked around the room, I approached a group of five kids who were reading the poems from *There Was a Place and Other Poems* out loud to each other. If one of them liked a poem, they placed an initialed Post-it Note on the page. I saw that there were already three or four initialed Post-it Notes marking poems. The teachers pointed out how this group of diverse kids, who weren't best friends, found something important they had in common with each other.

Some kids were sitting at their desks reading alone. Three boys were sitting cross-legged on the rug talking when I approached them. I asked, "What's going on?"

"We found our poems," one boy said.

"Already?" I thought skeptically about the possibility of them finding their self-portrait poems so quickly. "Will you read them to me?" All three boys had chosen poems from Lee Bennett Hopkins' *Click, Rumble, Roar: Poems About Machines.* The first poem, "Chant of the Awakening Bulldozers," began:

> But WE are the strength, not they, not they.
> Our blades tear MOUNTAINS down . . .

The second was called "The Power Shovel." I asked them, "Why, out of all the poems, did you choose these poems as self-portraits?" A small, thin-faced boy with very pale, almost translucent skin who was the spokesperson for the group said proudly, "Because all of our fathers are in the mining business and we're always around bulldozers and power shovels. The poems reminded us of our fathers." The poems they had chosen were self-portraits in that they reflected the love they felt for their fathers.

Next I talked to a girl who was sitting alone on the floor. She said, "My poem is 'crickets' by Valerie Worth, and the ending of that poem is like me":

> Crickets
> Talk
> In the tall
> Grass
> All
> Late summer

Long.
When
Summer
Is gone
The dry
Grass
Whispers
Alone.

When I asked her why she said, "Because last summer me and my friends had so much fun playing together, and then school came, and they either moved away or we had to go to school so we couldn't play anymore. Now I feel alone like the dry grass."

Tristan chose "The Kitten" by Ogden Nash as his self-portrait poem, and then wrote the reason why he picked the poem (see Figure 2–1).

Craig's desk was across from his friend Robert. Craig had short cropped brown hair and a round pudgy face. Robert had a long face and wore a base-

Figure 2–1 "The Kitten"

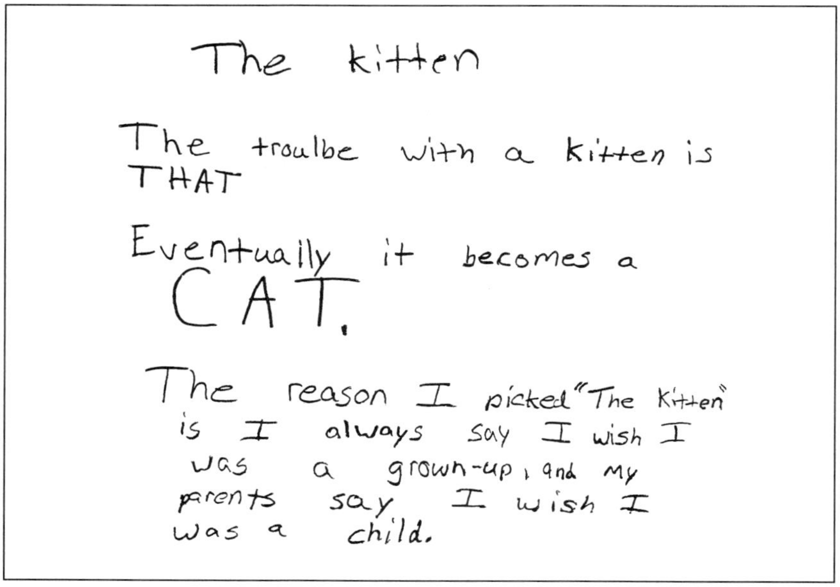
The kitten

The troulbe with a kitten is THAT

Eventually it becomes a CAT.

The reason I picked "The Kitten" is I always say I wish I was a grown-up, and my parents say I wish I was a child.

ball cap with a few hairs sticking out of the back hole. Craig was standing next to Robert, his elbows on his desk, quietly watching him copy "His Girlfriend," a poem from Myra Cohn Livingston's book *There Was a Place and Other Poems*. When I walked up, I looked over their shoulders. There were a few small Post-it Notes with their names written on them marking poems for possible second choices. They both had chosen the same poem. When Robert finished copying his poem, he handed the book to Craig to copy his poem. His teacher whispered to me that these two boys were best friends, but she didn't think that they had ever talked about their personal lives and the fact that both their parents were going through a divorce until now.

His Girlfriend
She smiles a lot.
She's pretty, I guess.
She tries to be nice,
but it's really a mess

to go out and have fun,
pretending you care,
laughing at jokes,

when your real mom's not there.

And then he wrote as his reason for choosing it, "Because I wonder about my Dad's girlfriend. She's OK but it's hard to like her." Craig chose the same poem and wrote something similar in his notebook.

My hunch had been right; by shifting the focus of the anthology project to poems that were mirrors of who the kids were inside, rather than what they liked, it gave deeper meaning to the poems and added a personal dimension to their search. Reading poetry is a social activity—a way of helping us hold hands with strangers who have more in common with us than we know. Poetry can give our students company and make them feel like they're not so alone.

After launching the self-portrait anthology project in many classrooms—and in all grades—I began to realize that I was losing an important opportunity to extend the project a natural step further. As the poets read their self-portrait poems, I discovered that a myriad of images, feelings, and thoughts about their own lives—the possible beginnings of poems—were appearing, especially as they wrote their reasons for choosing their self-portrait poems. For example, Matt chose a poem about stars as his self-portrait poem. He wrote as his reason:

> I like this poem because every star is different like humans. Also, there are millions and trillions of them. They age and live like humans and they die like humans.

What Matt wrote was the seed of a poem. I pointed this out to him, and read his own words back to see if he could hear the poem buried inside. He could. Then he played with the line-breaks to create a poem:

> Every star is different
> Like humans
> There are millions and trillions of them
> They age and live like humans
> And they die like humans

Later, I extended the self-portrait project by asking kids to illustrate images that the self-portrait poems helped them imagine about their own lives, and then write some words to describe these pictures. Often, their words were the start of poems as well.

Teshager, an eighth-grade student, chose "Final Curve" by Langston Hughes as his self-portrait poem:

> When you turn the corner
> And you run into *yourself*
> Then you know that you have turned
> All the corners that are left.

Beneath it he wrote: "I picked this poem because it reminds me of me. I still don't really know who I am." Then he illustrated a brick wall reaching from the top of the page to the bottom, a boy standing next to it, and these words:

> I'm turning
> the corner
> looking for myself.

After introducing the self-portrait anthology project in many classrooms I've gathered some important tips that have helped make the project run more smoothly:

- The key to the success of this project is to have a wide variety of poetry books accessible: nonrhyming and rhyming, silly and serious, poems about family, nature, animals, the city, poems that speak about different feelings, as well as poems spoken from varying cultural voices and experiences such as poems by Latino, African American and Caribbean poets.
- Be sure to choose poetry books relevant to your students' lives. Once I introduced this project to an inner-city eighth-grade class of mostly Spanish-speaking students, many of whom were members of gangs. The only books available were books like *Wee Willie Winky*, *Knock at a Star* by X. J. Kennedy, and Shel Silverstein. When kids began to read through the books their stereotypes of poetry were affirmed. I decided to postpone the project until the next day when I overhead one boy say, "I can't find my life in these books." The teachers and I desperately searched for books that were more relevant to their lives, books like *Cool Salsa* and *The Tree Is Older Than You Are*, which the kids read as if they were thirsty.
- Remind students to copy the poems exactly as they appear in the book—respecting the line-breaks and white spaces. Sometimes kids don't understand the concept of line-breaks—that the lines of a poem end that way deliberately—so students copy poems as paragraphs.
- Ask students to include the title of the poem, the poet's name, and the name of the book.
- Assure them that if they can't find a poem they connect to, they can keep looking, that it might take several days. We can also direct them to a particular book where they might be able to find one.
- Younger students who may have difficulty hand-copying poems can place a Post-it Note with their initials on it to mark the page where the poem is located for the teacher to copy in the copy machine later on.
- Suggest to students that they can copy excerpts or lines from a poem if only part of the poem speaks to them, or if the poem is too long to hand-copy in one day.
- As you travel around the room conferring with students be sure to help them understand a poem. Sometimes struggling readers will look at the title or the illustration accompanying the poem and choose the poem for this reason. It's a good place to start, but later we might set up reading partners for those struggling or early readers.
- For kindergartners and first graders, I suggest as I read a poem each day, during our ritual poetry reading time, that they listen for self-portrait

poems, and begin to collect these poems in their anthologies, and then write or illustrate why they chose the poem.

- Don't be discouraged if at first some kids choose poems too quickly or too literally. For example, one student chose a poem about chocolate ice cream because, "I just like chocolate ice cream." Read an example of your own self-portrait poem, and as kids begin to share theirs, other students will begin to catch on. Continue to describe why this anthology is different from others: that they choose poems to reveal or express something of themselves as a person—feelings, personality, passions, interests, and wonderings.
- The self-portrait anthology project can be a monthlong project or a project that takes the entire year where kids choose one self-portrait poem per month and create a portfolio of self-portrait poems for the end of the year.
- Include art. Kids can draw and paint their own self-portraits to accompany their poems. Show examples of artist's self-portraits to see how artists have expressed their inner selves.

CASEY

Casey was a foster child who was in Kathy Mason's loving first-second-third-grade classroom community in Arizona. When I visited Kathy's room I met Casey, who had the saddest eyes I had ever seen in a child. He was one of the children from whom I've learned an important lesson: that poetry can matter deeply.

In the afternoon, after the kids had searched for self-portrait poems, I noticed that Casey had slipped a poetry book inside his jacket as the children prepared to leave. I put my arm around him and told him that if he took that book home the other kids in the class who really needed that book too wouldn't be able to read the poems. I suggested that he copy the poems he felt were important into his notebook for safekeeping. Casey quietly reached in his jacket, took the book out, and said that he would copy his favorite poem into his notebook so he could have it with him. The poem he copied was "Help" by Myra Cohn Livingston:

> Help?
> Would it help
> if I could say
>
> *Don't worry, Mom,*

and if I pray
when Dad comes home
he'll want to stay?

Would it help?
No Way. No way.

Casey had discovered that poetry could provide some understanding and company with the difficult feelings he was having and felt so alone with. He and hundreds of other children are discovering the deep power, truth, and joy of poetry. Maybe that should be our goal: for every child to feel so connected to poetry that they too want to slip a poetry book into their jackets, to keep them company at home, and for all of their lives.

Layer Three: Guide students toward analyzing the craft of a poem, figuring out how a poem is built, interpreting what a poem means, or unlocking the puzzle of a difficult poem.

For many of us poetry has seemed like a door, locked tight with a chain and a heavy padlock across it. When we tried to open the door it wouldn't budge, because no one gave us a key to unlock it. Or we might have had a teacher who began to ask us questions about what's beyond the door. When we couldn't answer, our response was to run and never get near the poetry door again. Or we tried to bang against it, believing if only we could bang hard enough we'd be able to get in. And then when it didn't open we blamed ourselves—that we're not smart or educated enough—or we dismissed poetry as just too difficult and boring. These are feelings that many of us have experienced at some time or other and as a result never try to enter the door of poetry again.

When I read a poem I first let it affect my heart. My curiosity about the poem begins with amazement and love. And my eagerness to search deeper into analyzing a poem's craft comes from my yearning as a poet to know my craft better, so I can better express my heart.

Rather than standing up in the front of the room and asking questions about a poem I already know the answers to, I want to put my students in the position of learning about the poem for themselves. The key to learning how to enter the door of a difficult poem is to teach our students how to unlock the door themselves, and for them to find pleasure in this process.

UNLOCKING A DIFFICULT POEM

To read and understand the meaning of a poem takes patience. Sometimes it takes months, years, even a lifetime to completely understand a poem. Reading a difficult poem challenges us to read in a different way. We must learn to read a poem multiple times, and even then keep returning to it. It's a very different kind of reading than what most of our world demands—quick, easy sound bites to get us through the day.

Once I read about a man who was riding the subways in New York, and who came across the same poem displayed on the walls of the subway train by the Poetry in Motion program. He wrote, "It was on a Brooklyn-bound A train. I was reading the Emily Dickinson poem '"Hope" is the Thing with Feathers,' which is mounted in the train. I'd read it dozens of times. It had become routine—like reading the back of a cereal box. But I read it again, and—bang!—I got it. For a moment, everything was clear. Other things in my life, confusing things, also seemed to make sense."

- The more experience your students have in deciphering the meaning of a poem successfully, or to their satisfaction, the more confidence they will have.
- Choose a poem that's difficult to understand on first reading. Ideally, select a poem that you've read once or twice, and struggled to understand. By putting yourself in a similar position as your students, it will demystify the process for them.
- When you give a poem to your students, center it on a clean sheet of paper with a lot of white space around it so they can write directly on the sheet, or attach a blank sheet of paper beside the poem. They can circle important or difficult words, write questions about parts they don't understand, or just write their thoughts about the poem—making the poem more accessible and less distant.
- Ask your students to freewrite what the poem means to them—and circle or underline parts they don't understand.
- Ask them to talk to at least two of their fellow students—to see if a conversation with someone else can give them any further insights into their own understanding of the poem.
- Ask a few students at a time to the front of the class to give their interpretation of the poem and to ask the class any questions they might have. Encourage them to take risks in their interpretations and assure them that there will be no criticizing no matter how outlandish the inter-

pretation may seem as long as they can show where in the poem they got the interpretation.

- Ask them to take the poem home and reread it, then write another reflection about what it means.

After time spent reading, writing, and talking about a poem, multiple meanings will emerge.

CRAFT GROUPS: STUDYING HOW A POEM IS BUILT

As students find that poems can keep them company, and they begin to write their own, they'll begin to understand the architecture of a poem, or how a poem is built. One way to guide this understanding is to create craft groups—three or four students who study or focus on one poetry tool. Each group highlights and discusses one craft element, then shares what they have discussed with the rest of the class. There are many different possibilities for groups depending on the poem. Here are a few ideas:

- *Image:* Focus on the pictures the poet paints with words. Underline or highlight places in the poem where the words give a clear image. Identify parts of the poem where there are no images, and the poem is abstract. Illustrate an image or images and identify exactly which words help paint a clear picture.
- *Metaphor/Simile:* Underline words, lines, or phrases that surprise—that make the reader look at something in a new way. Which metaphors and similes are the most surprising? Why? Illustrate the two things which are being compared in a metaphor or simile.
- *Words:* Are there any words that surprise you? Which words feel exact and true? Which words add to the music of the poem? Circle unusual, strong, beautiful, and vivid words—focus on the sounds as well as the meaning. Why do you think the poet chose these particular words?
- *Line-Break/Stanza:* Discuss where and why the poet broke the lines of the poem. How does it enhance or contribute to the meaning of the poem? What rhythms do the line-breaks give the poem? Do the line-breaks help emphasize certain words? *Stanza* means "room" in Italian—is there more than one room in the poem? Why?
- *Beginning and Ending:* How does the poet open the door to the poem? Is the beginning an image? A surprise? How does the poet shut the door of the poem? Does the ending surprise you? Does the poem feel complete and resolved?

- *Music:* Highlight places where the poet uses sounds to glue the poem together musically: a chime, an echo, alliteration, repetition. How do the sounds contribute to the meaning and to the overall feeling of the poem?
- *Repetition and Pattern:* Does the poem repeat any lines, words, or phrases? Does it have a predictable pattern? If so, does the pattern change? How does the pattern contribute to the meaning of the poem?
- *Rhyme:* Highlight the rhyming words. Rhyming words can be at the end of lines or inside the poem. Are there any words that rhyme slightly (slant rhyme)? What is the rhyming pattern? Is the rhyming pattern consistent? Write the rhyming words down next to the poem. Do you see any meaningful connection between words? How does the rhyme contribute to the overall meaning of the poem?

After students meet in craft groups to focus on one poetic tool, they can then focus on another tool at another time. During our exploration of poetic craft I remind my students that craft cannot be separated from the meaning and feeling of a poem—that the purpose of each poetic craft is to express their feelings and experiences.

During this third layer of reading poetry we must keep asking ourselves the question: What will my students remember about poetry? Will they remember the *aba* rhyme scheme? Will they remember a poem's meter? Its similes and metaphors? Ultimately, I want them to remember a poem the way Mary Oliver does:

> But first and foremost, I learned from Whitman that the poem is a temple—or a green field—a place to enter, and in which to feel. Only in a secondary way is it an intellectual thing—an artifact, a moment of seemingly robust hardiness—wonderful as that part of it is. I learned that the poem was made not just to exist, but to speak— to be company.

3
Writing Poetry: Where Does Poetry Hide?

I've never heard a poet describe the origin of a poem by saying it came from an assignment about pretending to be a grass blade blowing in the wind, or from a poetry contest on health safety. Finding where poems hide for us is part of the process of being a poet and of living our lives as poets.

When I first began to teach poetry in the New York City schools sixteen years ago, I thought that the most difficult part of teaching would be to think of something "creative" for the kids to write about. I spent many hours planning "poetry starters" that would motivate: pretend you're a leaf blowing in the wind, write a poem from a part of your body's point of view. Once I assigned a poem written from their shoe sole's point of view about what they might see on the New York City sidewalks. I remember that day vividly. Some of the fourth graders diligently started writing while others took off their shoes, sniffed them, and threw them across the room. After a few minutes, the classroom was in chaos. And I remember thinking at the time, "Those New York City kids!"

What I hadn't understood yet was how uninteresting and perhaps even condescending my assignments were. If someone were to tell me to write a poem from my shoe's point of view, I might be tempted to throw my shoes as well. Discovering where poems come from is an essential part of a poet's process. I find my poems as I'm walking across Central Park on

47

soft rainy days, the rhythm of walking and the sound of rain releasing lines of poetry in me, or I find poems driving across the Arizona desert with the big sky surrounding me, or in the flashes of memory I have of growing up next to a creek in Virginia.

Poets find poems in hundreds of different places and ways.

Mei Yuan: "Only to be willing to search for poetry, and there will be poetry."

X. J. Kennedy: "Sometimes, when I wake up early in the morning, a poem will start waking up, too. That's a fruitful time, that half an hour in bed when I haven't yet shaken off dreams. A line of verse will come swimming lazily into mind, like a trout defiantly frisking its tail at a fisherman. . . . So, I figure I might as well just fool around with words and let an idea happen."

Lillian Morrison: "Writing poetry can be a way of pinning down a dream; capturing a moment, a memory, a happening, it's a way of sorting out your thoughts and feelings."

Myra Cohn Livingston: "Loneliness, a search for friends, alienation from others have always concerned me."

Stanley Kunitz: ". . . poems rise out of the swamps of the hind brain, 'the old brain,' dragging their amphibian memories behind them."

Robert Frost: "It begins as a lump in the throat, a sense of wrong, a homesickness, a lovesickness."

Where poetry hides

In Naomi Shihab Nye's wonderful "Valentine for Earnest Mann," the poem tells us that poems hide in unexpected places—often right in front of us in the everyday things and people in our lives. Poems hide for me in the oak leaves frozen in pond ice; in a spider's web hidden in the hole of a tree; in the sadness I feel at seeing a homeless person sleeping on the steps of a church. Naomi Nye writes:

> . . . poems hide. In the bottoms of our shoes,
> they are sleeping. They are the shadows
> drifting across our ceilings the moment
> before we wake up. . . .

W. S. Merwin's describes a similar idea:

> Inside this pencil
> crouch words that have never been written
> never been spoken
> never been thought
>
> they're hiding
>
> they're awake in there
> dark in the dark
> hearing us. . .

In Heather Getman's first-grade class in Scarsdale, New York, students had no trouble thinking of places where they could find poetry. One little boy, Eric, raised his hand and said, "Poetry hides for me in a walrus' mouth." What a fascinating place to find poetry! I certainly had never thought to look for poetry there before. I wanted to know more so I asked him, "Exactly where in the walrus' mouth does poetry hide?" He thought for a moment then said, "I don't know. But it also hides in his elbows."

Young poets have taught me that poems are all around if we are willing to search for them. The sparks of poems are not difficult to find as this poet showed when I asked him, "Where does poetry hide?"

> Poetry hides
> in music in the
> limbo
> Poetry hides
> in your shoe
> Where it walks
> Poetry hides
> in a clock
> in the numbers
>
> Poetry hides
> in a baby's giggle
> Poetry hides
> in a spring
> picture.

If they make a list, I ask them to star one item on their list where they could look even more deeply, and with more details describe where poetry hides (see Figures 3–1 and 3–2).

The doors of poetry

My nephew, Peter, who attends the excellent Manhattan New School, is a "poemmaker." Several months ago, Peter sent me the following list in answer to the question, Where do poems come from?:

1. Absorb. Be like a sponge. You can't just walk around and not notice things if you're going to write poetry. You have to notice everything.
2. Make things look different. You have to look at things in a different way—not the way you usually do.
3. Use 4D. When you write poetry you leave the three dimensions—and go to the fourth dimension.

Antoine de Saint-Exupery believes in Peter's 4D but he uses different words to describe it: "For behind all seen things lies something vaster;

Figure 3–1 "My backyard" list

*1. My backyard
2 Silver mines
3. Summer house
4. Hands
5. Cats
6. Band class
7. Grand father
8. Friends
9. Walls of my house

Wide open space
with a
    big blue
Sky in view.
There is green earth
everywhere.
Deep holes in the ground
dug with love, curiosity
and fur.
Long tatterd rope
rope hanging fron a
    beautiful tree
with swirling bark.
I have spent hours
runnig, playing in this
    dreamland.
When I step onto
it's magical ground
all worries fly
    away.

Figure 3–2   Backyard poem

everything is but a path, a portal, or a window opening on something more than itself."

The sources of poetry are endless. David Ignatow writes about keeping this window, portal, other dimension, or poetry door open, ". . . the door between the poet and words, so that words can come through." What are these doors? How can we help our students step inside? I usually begin by describing five doors that will invite all students to step over the threshold.

Poetry is the genre of the inner life, therefore, the first, and most important, poetry door is the door of our hearts. I encourage students to write
poems about what they feel is true. I tell them that their inner images
never lie, to trust those whether they be images of grief, sorrow, or rage.
That's the work of poetry—to give our inner images, longings, and feelings space to breathe. When Rita Dove, a former poet laureate of the
United States, was asked what she would like to accomplish as our na-
tional poet she answered, "I would like to remind people that we have an
interior life—even if we don't talk about it because it's not expedient, because it's not cool, because it's potentially embarrassing—and without
that interior life, we are shells, we are nothing." My students teach me
over and over again about keeping my heart open because that's where
the true source of poetry lies. Here are some examples of kids' poems
written from the heart. Sean wrote this poem on the birthday of her father, who had passed away:

The Birthday Without the Boy
We've got the balloons
We've sent invitations
We've got the confetti
We've got the cake
But now the ice cream's melting
Off go the lights
No more noise
Everything's ready.
Where's daddy?

Kevin writes "How My Mom Left":

My mom left long ago
We came here long ago
I look at the stars
I wonder which one
my mom lives on
I look at a big one
it fills up my heart
and that's the one
I think she's on.

THE OBSERVATION DOOR

The second poetry door is the door of our eyes—what we observe, what we're amazed by, what's beautiful in the world. Matthew Fox writes, "The kids I meet in school know that they're part of an amazing story: the universe story. They seek out beauty and mystery. You can hear it in their questions and in their poems." Poetry celebrates the world, and we write with a longing to know the world more deeply (see Figures 3–3 and 3–4).

THE CONCERNS ABOUT THE WORLD DOOR

Many kids think that the subjects of poems should only be love, flowers, or weeping willow trees. Poems can also be about what we read in the newspaper or about world events we watch on television—what we're concerned about: war, people who have to live on the streets, or floods in the Midwest. We can write a poem about the world in its entirety, not just the pretty parts; therefore, the third poetry door is the door of our concerns

Figure 3–3   "Settling Nightfall"

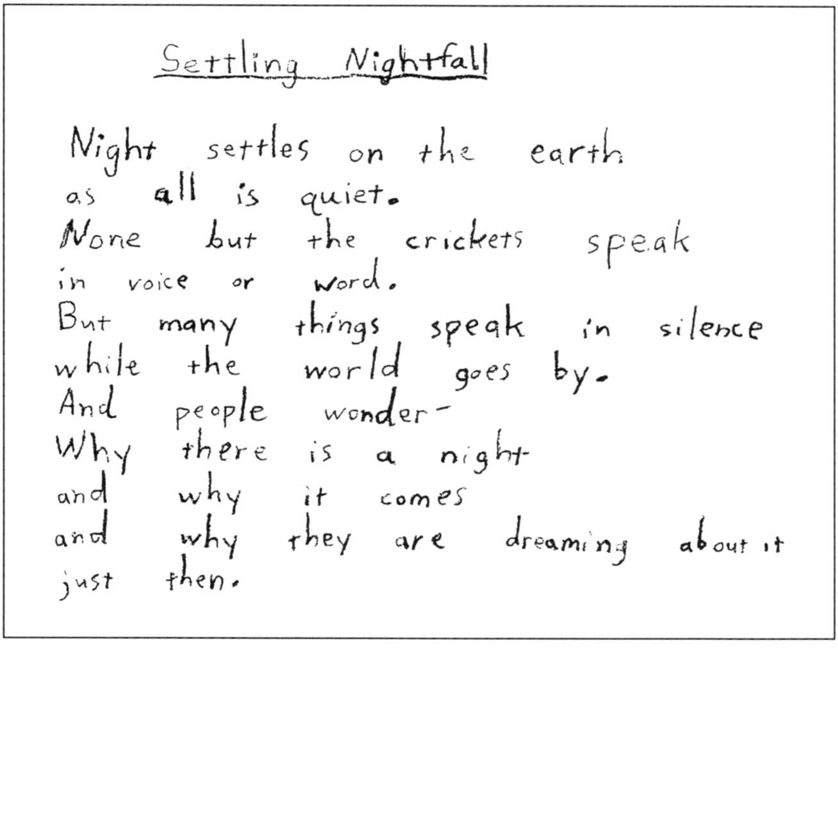

Settling Nightfall

Night settles on the earth
as all is quiet.
None but the crickets speak
in voice or word.
But many things speak in silence
while the world goes by.
And people wonder—
Why there is a night
and why it comes
and why they are dreaming about it
just then.

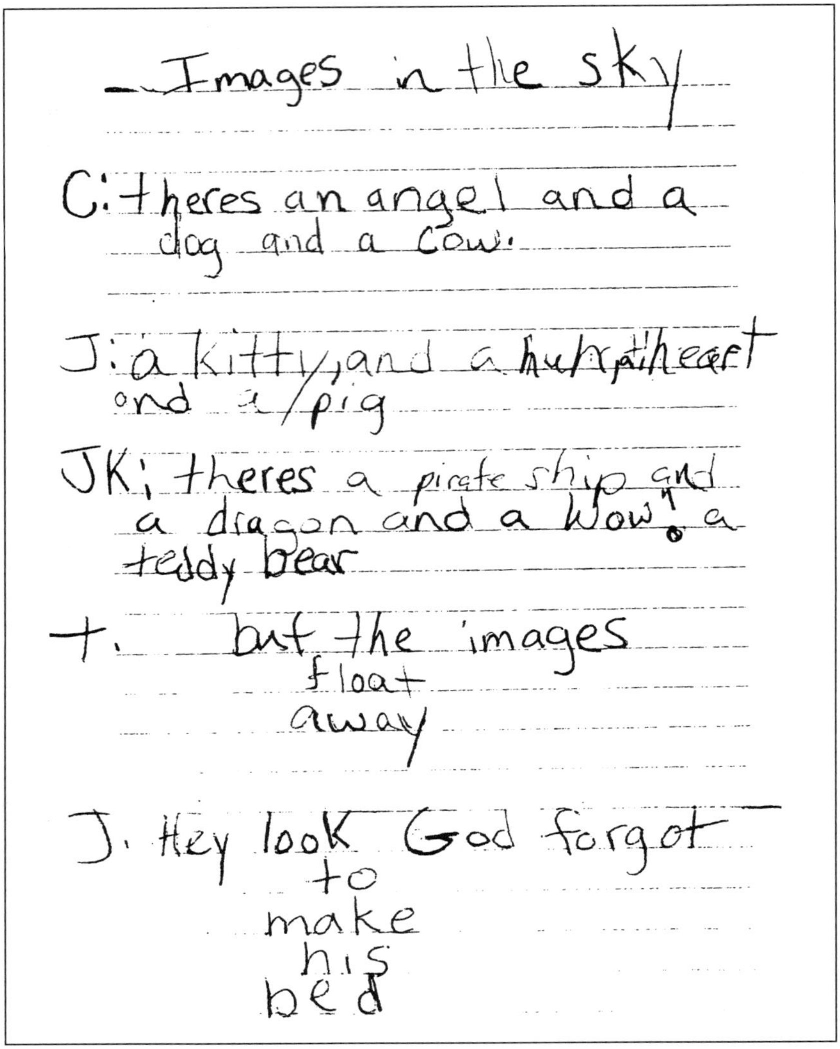

Images in the sky

C: theres an angel and a
dog and a cow.

J: a kitty, and a huh/a/heart
ond a /pig
JK: theres a pirate ship and
a dragon and a wow, a
teddy bear

t.   but the images
float
away

J. Hey look God forgot
to
make
his
bed

Figure 3–4 Poem for three voices

about the world. Poetry is about telling the whole truth of what we see happening around us. Matthew Fox understands this when he says "[Kids today] . . . are not in denial; they cannot afford to be. They know what is going on, what is happening to them and around them." Here are some of their concerns.

Pollution
One day the trees are going to disappear
and everyone would say I should have recycled.
Anyone would rather have a pile of gold,
than a rain forest,
later anyone would rather
see a rain forest.

The Homeless
Beauty in the world
Is almost done,
Beauty in the world
Is leaking through,
Love is soaring all around,
But in the wilderness
Some people wonder,
If they'll ever have hope,
The happiness is beyond their reach,
Love is still not done.

THE WONDER DOOR

Questions can be a lever for a poem. I ask kids if they have any questions about the world, their lives, what they're studying in school, the universe—whatever is unresolved or inspires their curiosity. Rilke wrote, ". . . be patient toward all that is unsolved in your heart and try to love the questions themselves, like locked rooms and like books that are written in a very foreign tongue . . ." The fourth poetry door is the door of wonder. I always tell my students that kids and poets are the most curious humans alive. Here is a question poem:

I Wonder??
I wonder where the frogs sleep,
and where they hide?
Maybe they are hiding in the water,
And they don't sleep at all.
I wonder what they just ate?
How do they communicate?
I Wonder

> When I die will I go to heaven?
> If I do, I wonder if I'll be a Devil or an Angel?
> Will Devils attack?
> Will I get to see God?
> Will I have a fishing rod?
> I Wonder
> How did the dinos die?
> Did a comet strike them out
> Or did a volcano spit?
> Did Food Town run out of food?
> Did they lose their fur coats?
> Were they rude?
> I wonder??

THE MEMORY DOOR

Stanley Kunitz said that we each have our own poet-in-residence in our minds—and that is our memories. Memories drift in and out of our minds all day long whether we are aware of them or not. The fifth poetry door is the door of memory. Although kids haven't lived as many years as adults, their memories are just as vivid and sometimes profoundly sad. In this poem, a student describes her experience of memory:

> Memories are stuck in your head like a
> seatbelt jammed between your car door.
> There are times of sadness that are
> contained in a bottomless pit in
> the back of your mind.
> You think of tears streaming down your face
> like little paced rivulets.

INFINITE POETRY DOORS

Finally, anything that doesn't fit into one of these five doors creates a new door. I hope that students will eventually know to write from, not just five but fifty doors—reflection, humor, dreams—the doors are endless. Every one of us should be able to step through at least one door to enter the world of poetry.

Where poetry hides for me

Sometimes I hear my poems into existence. A line will reverberate in my head, or a line in my journal will insist on being written down. It will have a family of words behind it, and it won't stop knocking until it is written. The poem "What We Hoped For" began with the line "sometimes I hear the wind in the trees . . ." I walked around all day saying it. I could tell that there were more words behind it. I waited until the spark was just right, wrote it down, and the poem came to me almost whole. My hunger in writing many poems is to understand. With this poem I wrote my way into acceptance and love.

What We Hoped For

Sometimes I hear the wind in the trees
and I think it's him come back
ready to ask the earth for forgiveness.

The smoke rises from the chimney.
It is late fall. All life has stopped
waiting for him to arrive.

I see him walking down the snowy driveway
to a house he never saw.

So much like the man I feared
when I was a girl.

Somewhere up there among the stars
is the way my life could have been.

My father circles with Ursa Major.
He has become part of the great spectacle.

We had a chance here on earth and what we hoped for
rises and sets with the sun.

Sometimes my poems are sparked by passion and concern, as with the poems in *Creatures of Earth, Sea, and Sky*. When I was in college I wanted to be a scientist—an oceanographer. The classes were conducted in a windowless auditorium consisting of hundreds of students. We never got to go outside, but instead had to memorize equations of waves breaking,

written on the overhead projector. I think it's because of this sterile, life-
less way of learning about the ocean that I decided to become a poet. But
many of my poems are fueled by that same scientific urge to observe and
know the world.

Dragonfly

It skims the pond's surface,
searching for gnats, mosquitoes, and flies.
Outspread wings blur with speed.
It touches down
and stops to sun itself on the dock.
Wings flicker and still:
stained-glass windows
with sun shining through.

A memory in the form of an image often triggers poems for me. This
poem and others from *Down by the Creek* comes from my childhood,
growing up next to a creek.

Wild Horses

My best friend and I
change into wild horses.
We gallop on lawns,
jump over fences
canter up hills,
slapping our rumps to go faster,
tangled manes flowing behind us.
We run toward the creek,
sip cold water,
and paw the grass with our hooves.
Then with soft tired whinnies,
walk to the deep pool of shade
beneath the tree to rest
and change slowly
from wild horses back into girls—
"But not any less wild," my mother says—
just in time for supper.

CREATING "WILD HORSES"

A poem's final form is inextricable from its revisions. It was in the revision process of "Wild Horses" that the poem became clear, and more like the experience in my memory. So the question "Where does a poem come from?" is answered more completely if we retrace the footsteps of making the poem from spark to raging fire, from memory to poem.

"Wild Horses" began as a memory, then became an entry in my notebook. The memory was as clear and vivid in my mind as if it were happening today. I often think of those hot, sticky Virginia summers when I was a girl where days were so long we didn't eat supper until late in the evening, and where I spent long hours playing horses with my best friend Mary. The memory was of us pretending we were horses, galloping around our neighborhood and doing what we imagined horses did. Although it started as a simple notebook entry, even at this early stage I felt the faint tugging of a poem.

Notebook Entry

My best friend and I used to pretend we were horses. We cantered up hills, jumped over fences and then went down to the creek to rest under the old tree—our hair tangled—sweaty—wild. Then I heard my mother call to come clean up for supper.

Next, I wrote the entry out on a separate sheet of paper to see if it really was a poem—and if so, how I could revise it.

Draft 1

My best friend and I used to pretend we were horses—galloping and cantering over our neighbors' lawns. We rested down by the creek, under the shade of the old tree. The shade was like our own pool. We sipped the creek water—mother called us to come home for supper.

When I definitely knew it was a poem I began to listen more carefully to the music of the words, I changed line-breaks, and "re-visioned" the memory.

Draft 2

My best friend and I changed
into wild horses. We galloped on lawns,
jumped over fences, and cantered up hills,

hitting our rumps to go faster, tangled manes trailing behind us.
We ran towards the creek
sipped the cold water,
and pawed the ground with our hooves.
Then with tired whinnies
walked to the pool of shade underneath the tree
to rest—and changed back into girls
just in time for supper.

"Wild Horses" went through several more drafts. Here are some of the revisions:

• I searched for more exact words:

Instead of *our hair tangled* I used *tangled manes* because it was more precise, and more in keeping with the horse image.

Rather than *we hit our rumps* I wrote *slapping our rumps* because *slapping* is more onomatopoetic (the sound of the word imitates the meaning).

Figure 3–5   Letter from young poet

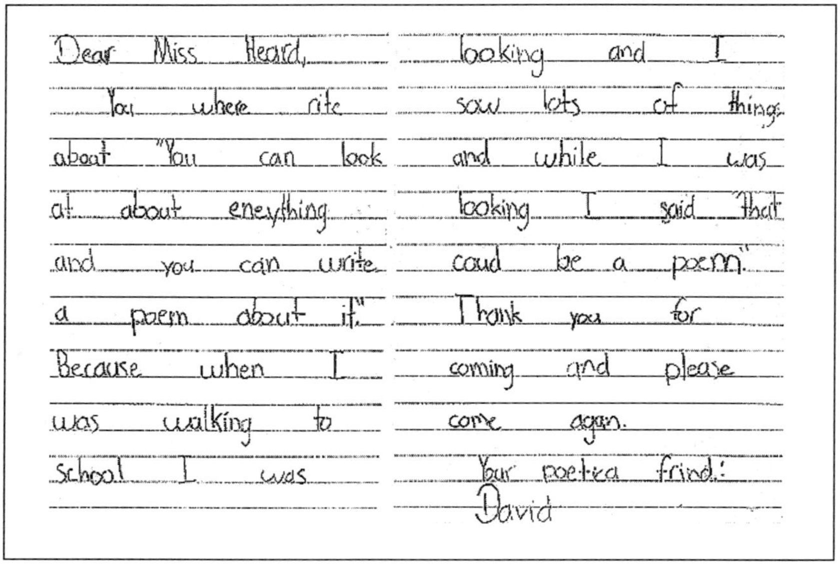

Dear Miss Heard,

You where rite about "You can look at about eneything and you can write a poem about it."

Because when I was walking to School I was looking and I saw lots of things. and while I was looking I said "That coud be a poem".

Thank you for coming and please come agan.

Your poetica frind:
David

I cut out the word *like* in the *shade was like a pool* and changed it to a metaphor—*deep pool of shade*—because it was both more concise and more accurate.

- I changed the past tense to the present tense so the experience felt more immediate.
- I rearranged the line-breaks by listening to the rhythm of my voice.
- The ending emerged when I remembered my mother's words *but not any less wild*, which gave the poem its resolution.

After a school visit I received a letter from a young poet who reminded me that I have done my job well if I can help my students see poetry everywhere (see Figure 3–5). A poem is born not because we willed it, begged it, or coaxed it with "creative assignments" but because when we begin to open our hearts and see poetry everywhere we are beginning to live our lives as poets. And, ultimately, that is where all poetry hides waiting for us to find it.

4
Crafting Poetry: Toolboxes

One of the academic initiation rites in my high school science classes was to take a frog floating in formaldehyde and dissect it with a scalpel. I remember that day well. I girded myself against feeling any pity for the poor frog; my goal was just to be able to get through it. What did I learn from this experiment? The truth is, not much. Dissecting a frog did little to further my understanding of biology or of the internal workings of a frog—if anything, it left an indelible memory of the nauseating smell of formaldehyde.

It comes as no surprise that when teachers tell me they dislike poetry they also tell me their primary experience with poetry was to dissect it in high school. To *dissect* comes from the Latin word *sicare, to cut*. To cut apart a poem in order to learn about what poetry is, is similar to—and as repellent as—cutting open a frog to really understand what a frog is.

Denise Levertov warns against this taking the life out of a poem. She says: "The would-be poet who looks on language merely as something to be used, as the bad farmer . . . looks on the soil merely . . . to be used, will not discover a deep poetry. . . ." The problem with studying the tools and craft that make a poem work is that because they are the most tangible, logical, and concrete parts of poetry it's tempting to remain there, ignoring the less tangible meaning that is at the heart of the poem—and is its life.

A few years ago, I met a teacher who was very upset because her middle school–aged daughter had burst into tears the night before over poetry.

"What's so bad about that?" I asked. "Poetry has moved me to tears many times."

"No," she said, "it's not the passion of poetry that made her cry—it was how it was presented." She handed me two sheets the teacher had given her daughter. It was the outline for the class' study of poetry. Page one consisted of a list of thirty-one poetry terms, which is not necessarily a bad thing to give to students, but it was how they were presented that was so daunting. The students were asked to write a poem, at least ten lines long, using at least five of these thirty-one terms. Toward the end of the two-page outline the teacher had written, "Your project will be evaluated on the basis of the following: Neatness—the entire notebook must be written in ink or typed. No spiral paper will be accepted." *That* was the only criterion. I smelled the formadelhyde.

How can the complex and emotional process of writing a poem be reduced to such formulaic simplicity? If students' first exposure to poetry consists of a sheet of glossary terms and labels most of them will have nothing to do with poetry again. A true understanding of poetry *cannot* emerge from the depths of students' souls and hearts if we begin with the labels and definitions of poetic terms. Many of us are cautious about approaching the part of poetry that opens our hearts, that lies at its crux—but we must first learn to take that emotional risk—with ourselves and with our students. It doesn't mean that we can't study the craft of poetry—all good poets know their craft intimately, and it is indistinguishable from the urgency and passion that calls a poem into being.

Grace Paley wrote, "I went to the school of poetry in order to learn how to write prose." If we teach the tools of poetry—such as image, choosing unusual words, metaphor, simile, and rhythm—then students' prose will improve because these same poetry tools are at the foundation of prose writing as well.

Poet comes from the word *poiein*, from the Greek *to make* or *to do*. Poets need to be masters of their craft, but only to serve the urgency of our hearts. A poet's job is to make experience, no matter how fragmented or unresolved, whole again in the act of writing a poem.

The meaning and music toolboxes

When I present poetic craft to students I keep two ideas in mind:

1. To introduce the tools not simply as terms with definitions but as vehicles that serve a more fundamental, deep, and emotional purpose. It is

how we present these tools, the language we use to describe them, that will make a difference to our students. How would a poet describe image, metaphor, or simile to another poet? What words do poets use? What's the feeling you get when you read a surprising metaphor or simile? Or are able to conjure the image of the poem clearly in your mind?

2. Introduce craft using the metaphor of a toolbox. A carpenter, like a poet, carries his or her tools to every job—nails, hammer, screwdrivers, chisels, bolts, planes, and level—just as a poet carries tools to the writing table. I see not just one toolbox, but two—which are equally important and have two different purposes in the course of making one poem. Just as a carpenter will reach for a screwdriver and a chisel, the poet may choose a metaphor and alliteration (see Figure 4–1).

The first toolbox is the Meaning Toolbox. It includes visual tools that serve to help the reader imagine, visualize, and ultimately, bring us closer to the experience of the poem. The second toolbox, the Music Toolbox, consists of those tools that help the reader experience the poem through sound, music, and rhythm. These tools fasten the poem together musically. In the actual writing of a poem, meaning and sound are inseparable, but for the purposes of trying to discuss some of these concepts I will consider them separately.

In the following pages, I've included exercises to help students learn and practice the craft of poetry. The purpose of the exercises is not necessarily to create a poem but rather to loosen up and expand students' poetic knowledge so that when they write poems it will be easier to express what they feel in their hearts. As a first-grade girl once said, "It's easy to say inside, and hard to say outside." The purpose of each exercise and poetic tool is to make what's inside easier to express on paper.

The meaning toolbox

IMAGE: MOISTENING THE POEM

When my grandmother died I wanted to write a poem about her. I tried, but all I could do was repeat my raw feelings—"I am sad. I am sad. I am so sad." After many tries I remembered a poem a third-grade boy wrote once about the death of his grandfather. The day Matt wrote this poem, I

Poetry Toolboxes
Tools to Help Craft Poetry

I	II
<u>Meaning</u>	<u>Music</u>
Expressing feelings and experiences through visual and sensory tools; revision techniques	Expressing feelings and experiences through auditory, musical and rhythmic tools
Image	Rhyme
Metaphor	Repetition/Patterns
Simile	Rhythm
Personification	Alliteration
Words	Words
Line-Breaks	Line-Breaks
Beginnings/Endings	Onomatopoeia
Titles	Assonance
Observation	Consonance

Figure 4–1   Poetry Toolboxes

simply asked the class to think of something that was important to them—a strong feeling, anything that was on their minds—and then to close their eyes and try to see a picture of it, to image or imagine it. I saw Matt close his eyes, and then he went back to his desk and wrote this poem, entitled "Pappy":

> I was very scared
> Hearing about my grandpa
> Going to the hospital
> It was a sad Christmas down in Florida
> When grandpa died.

I had a bad feeling
That when his ashes were buried
In a cardboard box
His ashes would be a part of nature
He would be a beautiful flower
But he would be trampled on
Like a bunch of weeds.

At the funeral
I saw Pappy floating up to heaven
Like a bunch of balloons
Our wreaths that were made out of
        pine needles
And put around his grave
Was like a last Christmas present.

Matt helped me remember my own images of my grandmother. We all have memories and images that we hold inside; writing poems allows us to explore them. If I say to my students, "Today I want you to find a representation through language of a sense experience," I don't think much poetry would happen. Rather than define image in glossary-like terms, I often quote what other poets have said about it—that's where the real heart and soul of poetry is. Poetry is about recognizing and paying attention to our inner lives—our memories, hopes, doubts, questions, fears, joys—and the image is the hook we find to hang the poem on. Many poets have expressed the power of image in passionate and beautiful ways.

Clark Strand: "Images bridge the gap between the particular and the universal, the inner and the outer."

Rilke: "Work of the eyes is done now/go and do heartwork/on all the images imprisoned within you." "The liberation of the poetic image is the releasing of the image from jail."

Stanley Kunitz: "One of my convictions is that at the center of every poetic imagination is a cluster of key images that go back to a poet's childhood."

Naomi Nye: "The energy that comes from rubbing one image against another in poems . . . we're desperate for that energy."

Wallace Stevens: "The greatest poverty is not to live in a physical world."

Robert Bly: ". . . the image moistens the poem."

In Marie Dionisio's seventh-grade class, I began introducing poetry by asking her students to think of something in their lives that they cared deeply about. "Whatever is on your hearts and minds: it could be a memory, or something you saw once that has stayed with you, or a feeling, or a thought. When you have an idea, close your eyes and try to picture it. Watch it until it's as clear as a photograph in your mind. An image is often a visual picture but you can use any sense—sound, smell, taste, or touch." I glanced around and saw that most of her seventh graders had closed their eyes; some were looking down at the floor. When I asked if anyone wanted to share, Jane Yoon raised her hand and asked, "What happens when all I see when I close my eyes is blurry?"

"Did you see anything at all?" I asked.

"Yes," she said, "I saw my grandfather. But I can't really see him because he's so blurry."

"This happens to poets all the time, Jane," I said, "sometimes it's in the writing of the poem that the image becomes clearer. Why don't you write down exactly what you just said, and explore the image of your grandfather even though he is blurred?"

Later, when everyone in the class had started writing I walked over to Jane's desk. She had written one page about trying to see the image of her grandfather, which was the beginning of a poem (see Figure 4–2). Jane's piece was powerful because she expressed her feelings through the blurred image of her grandfather.

Six-Room-Poem Rilke once compared writing poetry to "venturing into hitherto unexplained rooms." In Heather Byrn's fourth-grade class at the Punahou School in Hawaii, the students and I sat on the floor. I had never met any of them before, but I could tell that they took themselves seriously as writers because they carried their notebooks and pens with them—eager to take notes. I explained the idea behind the six-room-image-poem, and asked them to divide their papers into six boxes, or rooms (see Figure 4–3). I didn't tell them in advance what the six rooms would be.

"In the first room," I began, "I'd like you to think of something that you've seen outside that is amazing, beautiful, interesting, or that has just stayed in your mind. Now close your eyes and try and see it as clearly as a photograph—notice all the details about it—and describe it as accurately as you can. Don't think of writing a poem, just try to describe it and write your description in the first box."

<u>My Grandfather</u>

I just wish my pictures
were clear and then maybe
I could see my grandfather
and when I think about winter
when I think he is with me
I feel his hand touch my hand
it feels so cold like snow
I think he follows me everywhere.
I always feel sad when I
think of him because he died
when I was a baby so I want
to see his face I can't remember
how he looked like he seems
like hes water and then his
face in the water disapears. I
only feel him at night I
can feel him crying wishing I
could see him I wish I could
only see him again.

Figure 4–2   "My Grandfather"

For those few kids who looked stuck I suggested a few examples of images I had seen—Comet Hale-Bopp smeared in the night sky and a fiery sunset over the Pacific ocean. Giving them a window into my own images helped spark some of their own.

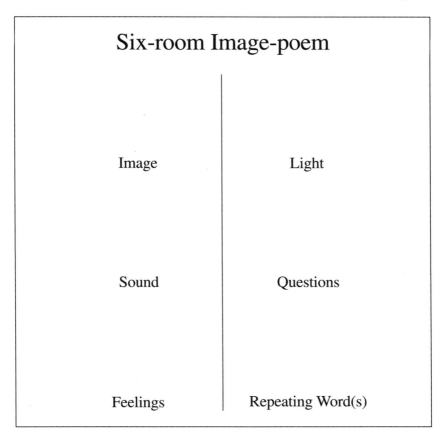

Figure 4–3   Image rooms

"In room number two, I want you to look at the same image as in the first room, but just focus on the quality of light. For example: Is the sun bright? Or is it a dull flat day? Are there any shadows? If it's unclear what the light is like you might have to use some poetic license and make it up. You can also describe colors. Or if your image is, for example, the stars, describe their light—shiny, sparkling, red, blue." I gave them about five minutes to write their descriptions.

"In the third room, picture the same image and focus only on the sounds: Are there any voices? Rustling of leaves? Sound of rain? If it's silent—what kind of silence? Empty? Lonely? Peaceful?

"In room number four, write down any questions you have about the image. Anything you want to know more about? Or wonder about?

"In room number five, write down any feelings you have about this same image.

"Finally, in room number six, look over the five rooms and select one word, or a few words, a phrase, a line, or a sentence that feels important and repeat it three times. I'll give you some time to read over what you wrote in the six rooms, then see if you can create a poem. You can re-arrange the rooms in any order, eliminate rooms, words, or sentences. Just try and create a poem."

For homework that night, Heather asked her students to continue work-ing and try to complete their six-room-image-poems. The next day she shared with me what her kids had written. Mark drew a picture of a house with smoke coming out of the chimney, and then read each room to create a whole poem. Figure 4–4 begins with the six-room exercise; Figure 4–5 shows the poem that emerged.

I've introduced this exercise in many different grades—and varied it from a three-room-poem to a thirteen-room-poem (like Wallace Stevens' poem "Thirteen Ways of Looking at a Blackbird"). Alyson wrote a mov-ing four-room-image-poem about her grandmother and labeled the rooms: Memory; Sound; Feelings; and Now (see Figure 4–6). Other suggestions for writing in additional rooms are:

- Think of three different similes or metaphors to describe the image.
- Describe any smells—earthy, sweet, damp.
- Describe what the image might feel like if you touched it. Again, use your imagination and make it up if your image is something like the moon or the night sky.
- Describe what your image would taste like.
- Take a favorite line or a quote from another poem or book and write that in one of the rooms to weave into the poem.
- If your image could speak what would it say? How would it sound? What would its voice be like?

This exercise is not necessarily meant to produce finished poems but to expand our vision of images for the next poems we write.

Exercise: Cracking-Open Words to Find the Image

Crack-open the sentences below by closing your eyes and seeing what images appear in your mind. Now repaint the sentences using your own images and words.

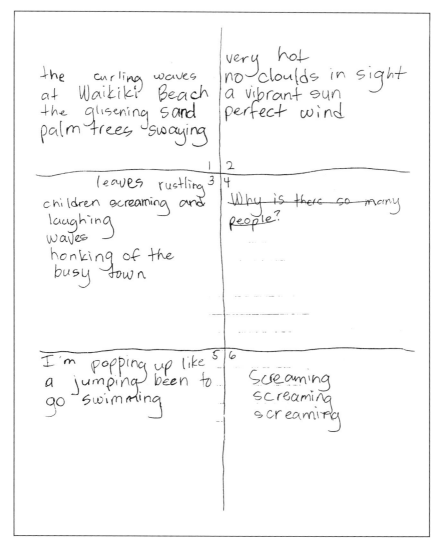

Figure 4–4   Six-room-poem

Example: *It was a nice day. = The bright sun, appearing from behind Mt. Chocorua, cut diamonds across the blue lake.*

It was a nice day. =

We had a lot of fun. =

Waves

The curling waves
at Waikiki Beach
glistening sand
palm tree swaying
It is very hot
no cloulds in sight
a vibrant sun
and a perfect wind
children
screaming
screaming
screaming
crashing of waves
children popping
to go
in the
water
Why
are
there
so many
torists???
torists??
torists?

Figure 4–5   "Waves"

The Star

Memory	Sound
my grandmother sick me waiting in my room you could feel the tenseness in the house eating away at her + my familes heart the disease was winning by lots	the sound of her screaming for help then the comforting voice of the man on the other line it will be all right it will be all right me running to her room the trucks the sirons then it was gone and went with her into bulding hoping she would come out.

Feelings	Now
me hoping to visit her but not getting to see her that night then she was gone hoping + praying to God I could see her again and I did in a coufin dead with no more love to give	flashbacks and her voice echoing in my head screaming for help just as she did her picture her wedding band is all I have left but I know that star outside my window is her looking over me still helping + loving me until I am gone to see her again

Figure 4–6   "The Star"

The flowers were beautiful and colorful. =

She was a good person. =

The cat was cute. =

METAPHOR AND SIMILE: THE LEAP INSIDE A POEM

The scientist Lewis Thomas wrote: "Children are the best of all at language. We are born with centers of some kind in our brains for making metaphors. We become specialized for this uniquely human function in the early years of childhood, perhaps losing the mechanism as we mature." If Lewis Thomas is correct, then our students should be teaching us minilessons about metaphor.

We hear kids speak metaphors and similes all day long in the classroom especially in kindergarten and first grade. In a first grade I visited, a bird had flown into the classroom window the day before and died. The class had a burial ceremony, and one of the first graders said, "And so I give to you this moth, to keep you warm and cozy down there with all the other birds."

One of the joys of metaphor and simile is that it gives us a "leap." Robert Bly says: "The real joy of poetry is to experience this leaping inside a poem." And Laurence Perrine writes, "The mind takes delight in these sudden leaps, in seeing likenesses between unlike things." Metaphor and simile are like windows into other worlds. They help us express our experiences in a new way—a comparison between two essentially unlike worlds.

Ordinary to Poetic The fourth-graders were gathered and I said, "One of the things that poetry does is that it helps us look at the world in a new way and describe it like no one has before. Today, we're going to write a poem together that tries to do just that. Let's look at something together—how about the trees outside the window here?"

I had drawn a chart next to me that had a line down the middle. On the top left I wrote the word *Ordinary*, and on the top right *Poetry*. I asked the kids to look at the tree and tell me the first words that came into their minds, adding that poets often begin their poems this way with "anybody's words." Under *Ordinary* the words they spoke were: green, tall, leaves, old. We read the list of words together and I said, "What do you think? Do you think it's a poem?"

"No. It's boring!" Jose said.

"This is what poets do. They write a few words down, and then they reread it and sometimes realize that they have to go back and resee. Now, let's look at the tree again, even more closely." There was a moment of silence as they gazed deeply at the tree. "What kind of green is it?" I asked. "The green of a frog? The green of the ocean? How old is it?" After a few minutes, they began to call out other ways of describing the tree. They spoke their lines to me, and I wrote down exactly what they told me:

Ordinary	**Poetic**
Green	Trees are as green as limes
Tall	Majestic giants
Leaves	Their leaves are jewels
Old	Historic recorders of time

We read the two versions and tried to understand together why the poetic side sounded and felt more like poetry. The words on the left were more generic words, and on the right they were transformed into poetry.

When they returned to their desks, a few students divided their papers into the two columns and wrote their poems that way (see Figure 4–7).

Figure 4–7   "Angelfish" Ordinary/Poetry

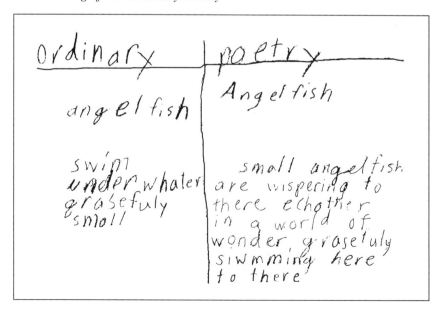

Sometimes we need to walk poets through what they do naturally but aren't aware of—like revisioning: the process of seeing again. We grasp for the best words to describe exactly what we see in our hearts by leaving one world and comparing or borrowing from another.

Exercise: Ordinary to Poetic

Choose one interesting object to look at—either out the window or in the classroom. Under ordinary *describe the object using the first words that come into your mind.* Then under poetic *transform these descriptions into poetry by using metaphor and simile or describing its exact details.*

Ordinary	**Poetic**

Finding Metaphors and Similes in the Everyday "Today we're going to try to write poems about the things all around us that seem ordinary but if we look hard and closely enough we can find the poetry inside." I held a safety pin up in my hand and said to the third-grade class, "You know it would be difficult for me to write a poem about a safety pin because it doesn't make my heart sing, and I don't have any strong feelings about it. But when I read Valerie Worth's poem 'safety pin' I'm able to see the poetry even in a safety pin. She makes me see this ordinary safety pin in a new way, and that's a poet's job: to help us look at the world in a new way. Listen to this poem that does just that."

safety pin
Closed, it sleeps
On its side
Quietly,
The silver
Image
Of some
Small fish;

Opened, it snaps
Its tail out
Like a thin
Shrimp, and looks
At the sharp
Point with a
Surprised eye.

The third graders sighed, and one boy yelled out "cool." Valerie Worth says:

> One of poetry's most wonderful features is that it can get beneath the surface of things and explore them not as mere objects but as remarkable phenomena with lively personalities of their own. Even such common articles as coat hangers can take on unexpected dimensions within the realm of a poem; and if this can happen with coat hangers, then the world must be filled with other "ordinary" subjects just waiting for poetry to come along and reveal their extraordinary selves.

One of the third graders, Emma, wrote about the zipper on her jacket (see Figure 4–8). Sarah chose to write about the little balls on her sweater:

Get Off My Sweater
I wish there were no little balls
on my sweater.
Wool threads that turn to balls
all the time.
Just picking them off
all the time
looking at them,
twirling them with
my pencil, they
just sit on my sweater,
doing *nothing!*
Not stopping pollution,
or eating,
nothing to do!
I wish they would
do *something!*
They could be
policemen,
dogs,
cats,
even mice.
If they would just
get off my sweater!

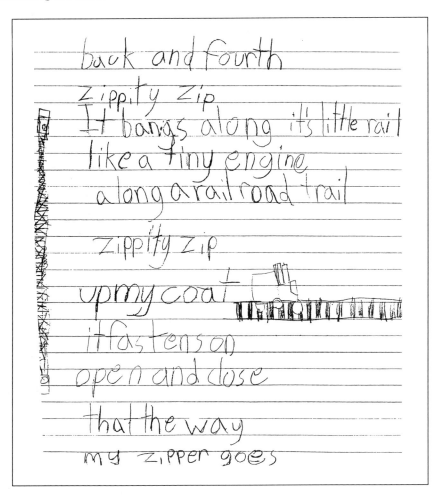

Figure 4–8   Emma's zipper poem

Spinning Metaphors and Similes As a way of "greasing the metaphor and simile wheel" I suggest my students think of several similes and metaphors when they're describing something. Pablo Neruda is a master at "spinning metaphors and similes." His poem "Ode to a Pair of Socks" describes a pair of socks as "two woolen fish . . . two gangly, / navy-blue sharks . . . two giant blackbirds . . . two cannons . . . two crusty old fire-men . . ." The litany of metaphors and similes, or what I call "spinning metaphors and similes," has the effect of spinning a kaleidoscope around to see the beautiful and multifaceted color variations.

To "spin" metaphors and similes you simply think of several different metaphors or similes about the same subject, rather than only one. Thinking of more than one metaphor or simile loosens your mind—and sometimes the most unusual comparisons appear. Here are some tips to keep in mind when thinking of metaphors and similes:

- Surprise your reader: "A rock is as hard as a pebble" is not surprising at all because the similarity of a rock and a pebble is too great. The linking of things that are both similar and different—such as a rock is as hard as a door, your heart, the truth—gives us more of a surprise.
- Don't be afraid to think of comparisons that may seem bizarre or unusual; if they don't work you can always take them out.
- If your subject is abstract like "love" or "justice" it's best to compare them with something concrete.
- If your subject is concrete (tree, desk, etc.) you can compare it with both concrete and abstract words.
- Take out *like* or *as* if not needed.

Exercise: Spinning Metaphors and Similes
Spin five or more similes for each below:

Love is like: **A giant oak tree is like:**

_____   _____

_____   _____

_____   _____

_____   _____

_____   _____

Extending Metaphors When I was a girl I was an ice skater. I spent every morning before school practicing my figures and free style. It wasn't surprising that when I wrote a poem about a mathematical compass I used a metaphor of an ice skater. To extend a metaphor is to stretch a metaphor out like a rubber band—writing only those details that connect to that one metaphor in some way. It's like a long gaze at something rather than a quick glance.

Compass
It stands
on bright silver leg,
toe sharp and pointed.

The other leg draws
a perfect circle
like a skater gracefully
tracing
half a figure eight
on paper ice.

Its silver skirt above
measures out inches

—two—three—four—

widening spheres
of mathematical perfection.

Figure 4–9 is a beautiful example of an extended metaphor poem about the moon.

Figure 4–9   "The Moon"

the Moon is a daddy
to the sun //
So when the moon //
has tucked in the sun
for tonight and
kisses his son // and says
sleeptight // the moon
takes over his son's
place // He Holds
the sky,

Exercise: Guessing Metaphors

Read the three metaphoric poems below. Try and guess what the title (the subject) of each poem is. Then try writing your own metaphoric poem.

_____ by Philip Dacey

The odd, friendless boy raised by four aunts.

_____ by Valerie Worth

Out of
Green space,
A sun:
Bright for.
A day, burning
Away to
A husk, a
Cratered moon:

Burst
In a week
To dust:
Seeding
The infinite
Lawn with
Its starry
Smithereens.

_____ by Charles Simic

Green Buddhas
On the fruit stand.
We eat the smile
And spit out the teeth.

(Titles to above poems: Thumb; Dandelion; Watermelon)

PERSONIFICATION: WHEN THE WORLD IS ALIVE

An eighteenth-century philosopher once said "It is characteristic of children to take inanimate things in their hands and talk to them in play as if they were living persons." To "personify" the world is natural for young children. I believe that poetry began when someone walked outside and saw, for example, the full moon rising over the sea, and didn't know about the phases of the moon, and thought the moon was a goddess emerging from the sea and thereby personified it.

Exercise: Personification

Go on a "personification" walk. Write down five things you notice— i.e., clouds, sky, leaves, grass, wind, and so on. Choose one and make a list of at least five ways your subject seems human or animal-like.
Example: Trees = Giant hands reaching toward the sky.

WORDS: THE POWER TO MAKE SOMETHING HAPPEN

Words are a poet's paint. Bobbi Katz writes: "I write poetry for the same reason I read it: the sound of words, their taste on my tongue, is irresistible. Words are the apple pie in my pantry that draws me out of my warm bed and sends me shuffling down the dark hall in the middle of the night."

When I speak to my students about words, I don't begin by talking about adjectives, verbs, and nouns; instead I try to share my love of language, and to give them the sense of what the Native Americans say, ". . . that every word has the power to make something happen." I keep a word notebook—a list of favorite words that I weave into my poems. The following poem written by a fourth grader is an example of one word propelling the poem into being:

Soccer
When I run,
I feel the wind
Bloom on my face

Sometimes I cover up the word *bloom* and ask kids to guess an unusual word they might use.

Exercise: Word Guessing

Fill in the blanks with the best words—be sure to consider image, meaning, and sound. Then look on the following page at the words the poet chose. How do yours compare?

April Rain Song
Langston Hughes

Let the rain _____ you.
Let the rain beat upon your head with _____ _____ drops.
Let the rain _____ you a _____.

The rain makes still pools on the sidewalk.
The rain makes running pools in the gutter.
The rain ___ __ ____ ___ ___ on our roof at night—

And I love the rain.

Compare the poet's words with yours. Why do you think the poet chose the words he did?

April Rain Song
Let the rain *kiss* you.
Let the rain beat upon your head with *silver liquid* drops.
Let the rain *sing* you a *lullaby*.

The rain makes still pools on the sidewalk.
The rain makes running pools in the gutter.
The rain *plays a little sleep song* on our roof at night—

And I love the rain.

Verbs: The Engines of Sentences Verbs are the engines of sentences, and the more abstract they are the less powerful the engine. In the first sentence the verbs are passive, and the power of the verb-engine is muffled. The second sentence has slightly more energy because *watering* is more precise than *doing*. But in the third sentence, we can feel the energy of the verb pulling the sentence forward.

1. She was doing something to the garden.
2. She was watering the garden.
3. She watered the garden.

The revision process includes cutting out excess words and sounds, and restoring the roar in a line or sentence.

Exercise: Verbs—Engines of Sentences
Of the list of these verbs—cut, sing, act, play, make, are, have, were—which ones give a more vivid picture in your mind? Which

verbs have more energy? Which is the engine of a fast car and a slow car?

Fast Car Verbs   **Slow Car Verbs**

LINE-BREAKS: SOUND AND SILENCE

My life in the city is filled with the sounds of people's voices, of cars honking on the busy streets, of fire engines and sirens blaring down Broadway. Several times a year, I drive up the highway and down several dirt roads to my mother's house in the middle of the woods in New Hampshire. The hardest thing to get used to when I first arrive in the country is its silence. At first it feels loud to me and more disturbing than the constant sounds of New York City but after awhile it feels blessed. Its presence is strong, as strong as the noises of the city.

It is this same tension between sound and silence that makes a poem. It is both the words—the voices on the page—as well as the silence between words that poets work with when we write poetry. Michael Harper writes: "The most important thing in a poem is silence. Yes, you know, *all* voids are not to be filled . . . some space has to be left there to resonate. It is often the *absence* of sound, what is *not* going on."

Think of the music of our own speech, our inner dialogue: we pause, we hesitate. When we write poems we must incorporate these pauses and hesitations into the structure of a poem. William Carlos Williams wrote these lines in his poem "To a Poor Old Woman." I like to listen to how changing the line-breaks emphasizes certain words and changes the meaning of one line:

> They taste good to her.
> They taste good
> to her. They taste
> good to her.

It is the line and where it is broken that helps make the music and rhythm of a poem. Generally, the longer the line, the more like natural speech it will sound. You can break a line:

- according to your natural breath
- to emphasize a particular word or words
- to counter your natural breath and to create tension
- to change the pace of the poem.

One line-break technique is called *enjambment*—when the break at the end of the line interrupts the natural rhythm or meaning of a line and is dragged onto the next line. Poets enjamb their poems for many reasons: to create tension; to disguise rhyme; and to vary the rhythm of a poem.

Exercise 1: Line-Breaks

Divide the following sentence in three different ways. How does the meaning of the sentence change depending on where the lines are broken? Try "enjambing" a line and see what effect that has. Which words are emphasized in each version?

> She loved the sound of the wind in the trees.

Exercise 2: Line-Breaks

Read the poem below and listen to the rhythm of the words: where does your voice naturally pause? Make slash marks with your pen or pencil to indicate the line-breaks. Try it two or three ways, then look at the original—why did the poet write the poem to look and sound like this?

Crickets talk in the tall grass all late summer long. When summer is gone, the dry grass whispers alone.

crickets
Valerie Worth

Crickets
Talk
In the tall
Grass
All
Late summer
Long.
When
Summer
Is gone,
The dry
Grass
Whispers
Alone.

ENDINGS AND BEGINNINGS: HOW TO ENTER
AND EXIT A POEM

How a reader enters and exits a poem is crucial to the life of the whole poem. How do poets open and close the door of a poem? Many of us are tempted to begin a poem with a story of how and why something happened. We often use too many introductory words. We must learn to trust the image and open the door of the poem on our most immediate experience.

Similarly, sometimes we are tempted to end poems by taking the easy way out—by writing in large letters at the bottom of the page "The End." Or we desperately end a poem by summarizing, "And we had a lot of fun." Some poems end by returning to the beginning, repeating the first line, like a snake with a tail in its mouth; some begin and end with a bang, a surprising image or metaphor; some poems begin with an emotional statement or end with a clarifying statement such as Rilke did at the end of a poem, "I must change my life." (See the Beginnings, Endings, and Titles exercise below.)

TITLES: NOT JUST A LABEL

Titles are not just labels slapped on the top of a poem like on cans at the grocery store: ketchup, bread crumbs, paper towels. A title is an intricate part of the overall texture of the poem. Titles can add another dimension to a poem, give it a double or symbolic meaning, act as the first line, or surprise the reader.

Exercise: Beginnings, Endings, and Titles

Read the poems below. Notice how they begin and end. How do the titles contribute to the meaning of the poems?

Poem

Langston Hughes

I loved my friend.
He went away from me.
There's nothing more to say.
The poem ends,
Soft as it began—
I loved my friend.

Foghorns
Lilian Moore

The foghorns moaned
            in the bay last night
so sad
so deep
I thought I heard the city
            crying in its sleep.

Keepsake
Eloise Greenfield

Before Mrs. Williams died
She told Mr. Williams
When he gets home
To get a nickel out of her
Navy blue pocketbook
And give it to her
Sweet little gingerbread girl
That's me

I ain't never going to spend it

Suspense
Debra Chandra

Wide-eyed
the sunflowers
stare and catch their summer
breath, while I pause, holding basket
and shears.

This Is Just To Say
William Carlos Williams

I have eaten
the plums
that were in
the icebox

and which
you were probably
saving
for breakfast

Forgive me
they were delicious
so sweet
and so cold

The music toolbox

I look at the tree outside my window. A few leaves are tenaciously hanging on through November. As I'm writing I see them flutter as the strong north wind whips at its branches. I'm reminded of Langston Hughes' idea that there is rhythm everywhere and in everything. There's rhythm in the way the tree blows back and forth, in the movement of those few leaves, and in the way we all speak. Even without words the world has rhythm.

The dimension of sound in a poem is usually not obvious to kids unless the poem has a definite and strong rhyme, pattern, or beat. By learning to use the proper tools we can create an awareness of the sound and music in a poem, even if that sound is subtle. Every poet uses sound and music when reading or crafting a poem. Donald Hall writes:

> I say you read poems with your mouth, not with your ears, and they taste good. When I read a book silently, sitting in my chair, my throat gets tired. My mouth is really working, chewing on these sounds.

And David Mura says:

> When I talk about writing poetry with students, I tell them not to go in a straight line and not to think what they would logically think. Then the question becomes, How do you proceed in a non-logical way which lets your imagination and your unconscious out? Associate through sound.

How do we "associate through sound"? We want our students to taste the sounds of words in their mouths, to hear the subtle echoes of less obvious rhymes, to hear the effects of a poem with a lot of hard consonants or soft vowels. Sound is perhaps the most abstract dimension to teach, and yet music, rhythm, and sound are the first things young children respond to in a poem. The love of sound exists from an early age.

There are a myriad of ways to fasten a poem together musically. All of them are a form of repetition. Hearing the same sounds over again creates a music that borders on song. Here are a few of the most frequently used musical tools:

Rhythm (the music of the words in a line)

Repetition (repeating words, phrases, lines, or groups of lines)

Rhyme (rhyming words within the line are called *internal rhyme* and rhyming words at the end of a line are called *end rhyme*)

Alliteration (the repetition of initial consonant sounds, as in *meaning* and *music*)

Assonance (the repetition of vowel sounds, as in m*ou*th and h*ou*se)

Consonance (the repetition of consonant sounds, as in *short* and *sweet*)

Onomatopoeia (words that sound like what they mean, as in *bang* or *slap*)

When a poem or a line has soft, pleasant sounds (which means it has a lot of vowels) we say it is *euphonious*, when a poem or a line sounds rough or sharp (it has a lot of consonants) we say it is *cacophonous*.

Exercise: Fastening the Poem Together Musically
In the following poems highlight the places where the poem is fastened together musically. Try to identify which musical tools the poet has used.

> Pease porridge hot
> Pease porridge cold
> Pease porridge in-the-pot
> Nine days old.

Wind Song (Excerpt)
Lilian Moore

When the wind blows
the quiet things speak.
Some whisper, come clang,
Some creak.

Eagle Flight
Georgia Heard

Eagle gliding in the sky,
circling, circling way up high—
wind is whistling through your wings.
You're a graceful kite with no string.

Exercise: Drawing Sounds
Each word is its own musical instrument. Illustrate the sounds of the following words, not *their meaning. For example, the word* hour—I *wouldn't draw a picture of a clock or numbers—instead I listen to the sound of the word and hear its soft sounds and that it has no sharp or hard sounds, so my illustration might be a curved line— like the curve of a half moon to illustrate this softness. Or you can choose words out of the dictionary that your students don't know the meaning of, which will help them separate the meaning of the word from the sound.*

glide

peek-a-boo

solar system

ax

Exercise: Word Textures
Next to each word-sound description write a list of words that match the texture of the word-sound. For example, two smoothly textured words are ice *or* rise.

Smooth (For example, *slice*)

Bumpy (For example, *hippopotamus*)

Hard (For example, *catch*)

No matter what tools we teach our students to use we need to remember that the ultimate goal of teaching craft should be a heartfelt poem that is

the expression of beauty, something that helps us through the humdrum day, something that shocks us out of ourselves and something that makes us believe in the beauty and the glory of human existence.

5

Sharpening Our Outer
and Inner Visions:
Poetry Projects

Several years ago on the Fourth of July my sister and then five-year-old nephew, Peter, came for a visit. It was a sticky July evening and after dinner my sister and I were talking about many things, including how the slugs in the backyard were eating my tomatoes. Peter sat quietly in his chair, listening intently. Suddenly, he burst out, "I don't want to go see the fireworks, I want to watch the slugs." My sister and I looked at one another, surprised, but she said OK, and I agreed to stay home with Peter.

Everyone left to see the fireworks, and Peter and I prepared for slug viewing. He dressed in his pajamas, we tiptoed outside breathing the sweet night air and took our spectator seats on the back steps. We waited for what seemed like a long time, and Peter began to worry that we might have scared the slugs away. Finally, one plump slimy slug glided slowly out of the porch crack. Peter climbed in my lap. "Can I touch it?" he asked and reached his finger out toward it. When he touched it, Peter squealed, "His horns are going in," and snuggled deeper. We watched the slug ooze down one step, then another, the porch light a spotlight for our viewing. We whispered to each other, "Look at its striped back. It looks like a cow. Look at the silver trail it's leaving behind." Peter had many questions. "Do slugs have eyes?" he asked. We bent our heads closer but didn't see any. "How does it move?" Neither of us were slug experts so we just watched and, after a while, our slug disappeared into the grass. It was time for Peter to go to bed, and for the slug to move out into the night and destroy my tomatoes!

What Peter taught me that night is what children do for adults all the time; they help us see the beauty in things that we no longer see, that have been obscured by a film of familiarity. I never bothered to stop, or wanted to look with appreciation at slugs. Peter taught me that there *was* a kind of beauty in them. The way he talked about them was the talk of someone who is seeing the slugs for the first time and, ultimately, the language of poetry.

Most children study the world with the intensity of scientists, and in their seeing they help us see things we have never seen before. This is also a poet's job—to observe carefully and then to find words to express what we see. But we must learn to observe in detail with our eyes *and* our hearts; we must sharpen both our outer and inner visions.

Pablo Neruda wrote about two kinds of poets: the poets of closed rooms, who write mostly about their inner feelings and lives; and the poets of the open windows, who write from what they observe in the outside world. Clark Strand also wrote about the importance of poets paying attention to both visions: "If we only understand looking out, our poems will have no heart. If only looking in, they are likely to become self-indulgent or obscure."

As I work with students, I keep these two goals in mind: to help guide them in sharpening their outer vision as well as their inner. Therefore, this chapter has two sections: the first describes ways to guide our students in honing their outer vision through observation, sketching, and field journals; the second focuses on helping students sharpen their inner vision by heart mapping and finding their inner poet. By alternating these visions, I hope that the poems the kids write will show an integrated vision of the world.

Sharpening outer vision: the power of observation

Pablo Neruda wrote, "You not only have to open the window but come through the windows and live with rivers and animals and beasts. I would say to young poets . . . to discover things, to be in the sea, to be in the mountains, and approach every living thing." Observation is an essential tool of poets and scientists. Ezra Pound expressed a similar idea, "The proper METHOD for studying poetry . . . is the method of contemporary biologists, that is careful first-hand examination. . . ."

I encourage my students to become open-window poets—especially if they live in the city. Those rivers and animals and beasts Neruda spoke of are trees lining a street, pigeons roosting high up in the arc of a window, or all the different faces we see as we walk along the city sidewalk.

One day last fall, Peter, who is now in third grade at the Manhattan New School, took an observation walk with his class. The school is located in the heart of the city where there are no huge meadows filled with wildflowers and little wildlife. They were asked to choose one thing to observe and write a poem about. At first, Peter said he looked and he couldn't see anything that interested him to write about. And then, "All of a sudden I looked and saw a tree that looked like a giraffe." And he wrote "A Tree" (Figure 5–1).

If we look hard enough we can always find amazing things to observe and write poems about no matter where we live.

Figure 5–1 "A Tree"

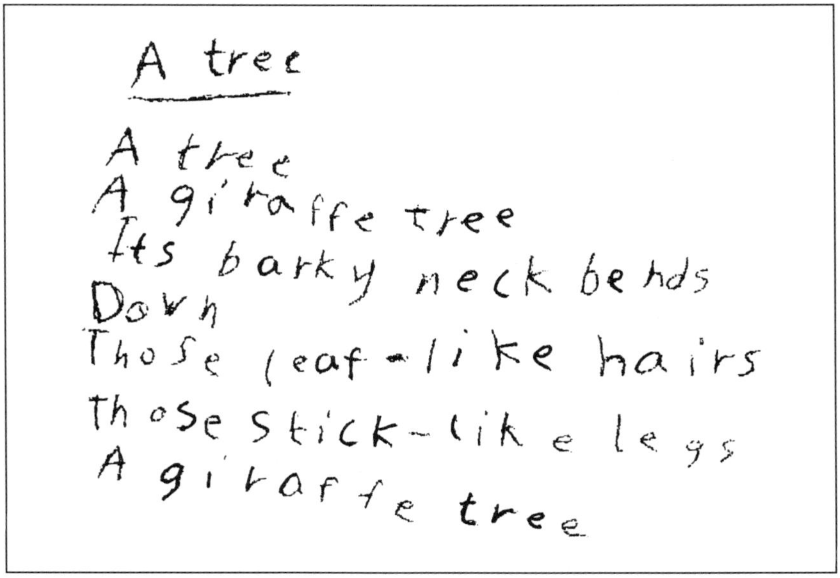
A tree

A tree
A giraffe tree
Its barky neck bends
Down
Those leaf-like hairs
Those stick-like legs
A giraffe tree

OBSERVATIONAL DRAWING

In order to nurture the scientific observer in every poet I began a project in a fourth-grade class. I wrote them a letter:

> Dear Poets,
> Please bring in a beloved object from nature—an acorn, a shell, a nest, a bone, a shark's tooth, a piece of pine, a flower—some piece of nature that you've chosen because you think it's beautiful, makes you wonder, or amazes you. It should be carefully selected as a reminder of the beauty and the vastness of the natural world. Whatever you choose, it should have a story, a wonder, or a memory attached to it.

When the kids brought in their beloved objects I could see that they had chosen them with care: acorns, seashells, pieces of bark, a sand dollar, and other treasures were wrapped in tissue and carefully placed in plastic bags and shoe boxes for safekeeping. I brought in some extra shells for those who might have forgotten to bring in something. We gathered together in the back of the room to talk about what treasures they had brought in. Michele brought in a twig from the tree in her backyard and said, "This is the tree that I see every day, and it means a lot to me because it's like a person—it's filled with so many memories." Janine brought in a large conch shell her father had given her and when she placed it over her ear she could hear the same ocean that he had heard. Chris brought in a nut and a piece of pine tree and asked, "How much magic can the world hold for us?" As we talked about the beauty of a gourd, the color of a leaf, and a bird's nest—all reminders of the big earth—even our talk sounded like poetry.

Next, I read Karla Kuskin's wise advice to poets:

> One aspect of a poet's life is really seeing. . . . If you are going to draw, you have to look at that leaf and see the way the lines come down. You have to see the way the leaf is shaped and the way each plant grows differently. When you're drawing, you're drawing details, that's what you're writing about, too.

Inspired by Karen Ernst's work with art and writing in her wonderful book, *Picturing Learning*, and from my own experiences, I've learned that drawing helps me really see the details of what I'm looking at. It's a good technique for helping our students to linger when they observe—to encourage the eye to saunter rather than to glance quickly. If we ask our students to write with details, we must first teach them to notice the details.

That day, I asked my students to make several sketches and to notice the smallest details of their pieces of nature. When they returned to their desks, they posed their objects. A few kids exclaimed that they didn't know how to draw. I reminded them that it was just a sketch, and the point was not to make perfect drawings, but to really see. As I walked around the room, I noticed that everyone had begun to draw. I stopped next to Andrew, who was drawing a nut, and I asked him what he was noticing. He said, "It's like a little boat." Michael, who was sitting next to Andrew, said, "I never knew that a pinecone was like a little house with all its windows open." And Jody, who was drawing a feather, said "I feel like I'm really touching it in my hand by drawing the picture." Before we gathered for sharing, I asked them to write down the details they observed that they hadn't noticed before sketching their objects.

At our sharing time, most kids were amazed at how much the drawing had helped them become better observers. I read them one of my favorite quotes by Frederick Franck:

> Once we start to draw, all of a sudden we begin to see again. Were we blind? How could we have ignored the beauty, the intricacies of these "simplest things," the convoluted network of veins in an oak leaf, the graceful curve of a clover's stem, the starry splendor of a humble dandelion, the voluptuous curves of a green pepper? How could we have missed the ardor of that little twig wresting itself free from its mother branch? In the course of a few hours the capacity for wonder is restored, with new awe for the gift of seeing we had forgotten.

As they shared, I took notes and I realized that observational drawing could help my students' poetry in many ways:

- Drawing helps them to linger, to slow down, and to stay with seeing and reseeing (revisioning), which is at the heart of all writing.
- Drawing also encourages them to notice details they might not have noticed before.
- Drawing sharpens their visual sense, which will help them write more concretely and with images.
- Drawing natural or ordinary objects helps them see poetry in the ordinary, small, and unglamorous.

As I listened to them share, I noticed that their words sounded like poetry. I thought of Thoreau who wrote in his journal:

I have a commonplace book for facts, and another for poetry, but I find it difficult always to preserve the vague distinction . . . for the most interesting and beautiful facts are so much the more poetry. . . . They are translated from earth to heaven.

The next day, with Thoreau's words in mind, we wrote a class poem to help transform their observations into poetry. We made an Earth to Heaven chart (similar to the Ordinary to Poetic chart described in Chapter 4). At the top of the chart, on the left side, I wrote Earth—under this column we wrote observations—and on the top right side of the chart I wrote Heaven, beneath which we transformed some of these observations into poetry. Later, when the kids wrote their poems, I was amazed at their powers of observation and their poetry. Ricardo created an Earth to Heaven chart on his paper as he was looking at a seashell:

Seashell

Earth	Heaven
Big	The shells make life
Rough	come back.
Hard	And people that
Soft Inside	collect shells
Skeleton	must shine
Hear the sea	in the dark.

Amy's drawing of a butterfly wing helped her to write this poem:

Blow on it, it will flutter in place.
Rub on it, it will lose its color.
Drop it, it will do flips and turns.
Bend it, it will lose its life.

And after Greg sketched he discovered a world of poetry inside his shell:

Shell World

Inside a shell
you can hear
magic waves
on the mystic shores
of the shell world.

Transforming Observations into Poems   As we read poems, the kids noticed that there are many different ways poets transform their observations and facts into poetry. We began to make a list of some of these (Figure 5–2):

Reflections and thoughts: What are you thinking about as you observe?

Lists: Describe and list the details you notice.

Metaphor and Simile: What does your object look like or remind you of? Spin a few metaphors or make an extended metaphor.

Questions: What are you wondering about?

Feelings: What feelings do you have about what you're observing?

Memories: Does it remind you of anything in your own life?

The Larger Picture: What's the larger context? Where did the object come from?

If we can teach our students to really see maybe those powers of observation will be with them the rest of their lives, and they'll be able to transform whatever their lives give them from ordinary to extraordinary and, ultimately, from earth to heaven.

POETRY FIELD JOURNALS

It was a windy but mild day in October when Irene Tully's twenty-two fifth graders, spiral notebooks and pens in hand, first walked down the

Figure 5–2   Observation

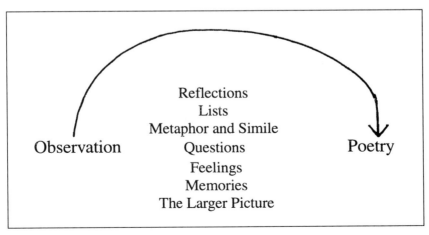

Observation

Reflections
Lists
Metaphor and Simile
Questions
Feelings
Memories
The Larger Picture

Poetry

road to Pussy's Pond in Springs, New York, a rural community two hours east of New York City. The kids were talking and laughing on the way—happy to be out of school on such a beautiful day.

Irene began the year by testing her belief that like Thoreau, if her students really learned to see and observe the world around them, they would experience the world more completely, and this would help them become better poets and writers and, perhaps, more concerned citizens of this planet. In September she began by reading aloud excerpts from Thoreau's journal as well as from what Pablo Neruda called "open-window" poets like Mary Oliver, Gary Snyder, and Valerie Worth.

Thoreau, who lived in solitude on Walden Pond for years, kept a journal to record his observations. He trained himself over many years to see the world around him. His neighbors often saw him standing beside a pond—sometimes for eight hours—to watch frogs, or by a river to watch duck eggs hatching. Emerson said of Thoreau, "It was a pleasure and a privilege to walk with him. He knew the country like a fox or a bird. . . . He knew every track in the snow or on the ground. . . . Under his arm he carried an old music-book to press plants; in his pocket, his diary and pencil, a spy-glass for birds, microscope, jack-knife, and twine. [He] read the names of all the plants that should bloom on this day. . . ." He wrote in his journals at least two to three hours a day, and they are thick with observations:

April 16, 1852

As I turned round the corner . . . saw a woodchuck, the first of the season, in the middle of the field . . . I squatted down and surveyed him at my leisure. . . . The head between a squirrel and a bear, flat on the top and dark brown, and darker still or black on the tip of his nose. The whiskers black, two inches long. The ears very small and roundish, set far back and nearly buried in the fur. Black feet, with long and slender claws for digging. . . . We sat looking at one another about half an hour. . . . I saw that by so much gritting of the teeth he had worn them rapidly and they were covered with a fine white powder. . . . I spoke to him kindly.

Irene also read poems and excerpts by Mary Oliver, who spends part of each day walking the shores and marshes near her home:

I have a notebook with me all the time, and I begin scribbling a few words. . . . I think our duty . . . as writers begins not with our own feelings, but with the powers of observing, and so I may get some words which describe, though I don't know at the time where they're going to move from that. I do have a little notebook, and Provincetown is where I live really privately, and where I walk a lot. Once I was in the woods and I had no pen, so later I went around and hid pencils in some of the trees.

Like Thoreau and Mary Oliver, Irene's students carried their spiral observation journals wherever they went.

Throughout the year Irene and her class walked to the nearby pond to observe and record what they saw. On this particular day in October, a group of boys were the first to walk along the edge of the pond. They suddenly stopped, crouched down, and whispered to Irene and the rest of the class to come see. They had spotted a blue heron, hidden in the reeds. Everyone tiptoed quietly over to where the boys squatted, but the commotion startled the heron. It rose in the air, and they heard the whishing of its wide wings as it flew up and over the pond.

Irene said, "Quick! Write down what you see and hear so you won't forget it." After that initial sighting and excitement, the class settled down. Some stood quietly, searching the reeds for more heron, others sat on the ground staring at first, and then began to write. The wind whistled and they could hear the rush of grass blowing.

Later, Irene told me, "That was the hardest part—that first week or so. Fifth-grade kids aren't used to standing in one spot for very long, and really looking. Just like Thoreau had to teach himself to see, my job is to teach these kids to really see."

In April Mike wrote in his journal:

April 7th

Last night I went to a blue spotted salamander walk. I saw two blue spotted salamanders and two spring peepers. The blue spotted salamander only lives in two places in the world—Montauk and Prince Edward Island. (There is also supposed to be some in Connecticut).

April 20th

Yesterday in school our class went to Landing Lane. We saw 9 snowy egrets, 5 ospreys, and 1 great blue heron. 1 of the ospreys was flying proudly staring at me. We had a great time.

After a few weeks of keeping observation journals, Irene and her students reread their field journal entries, searched for the beginnings of poems, and wrote poems from these observations. Her hunch was right: observation had made a difference and had revealed itself in their poetry. Irene was amazed by the specificity of observation in their poems:

Landing Lane
Alyssa Forlenza

The wrinkled
water
tells old
stories to
the
birds
who fly
above.
The mellow breeze
calms me. The wrinkling
water hypnotizes me.
The swaying grass tells me
a story.
A boat
carefully
listens to
the wind's
favorite
stories.

Irene said that, yes, the field journal observations had changed their poetry—but would it make a difference in their lives, and how they saw the world outside of school? She became convinced it would when she heard that four of her boys—Mike, Hoker, Nathan, and Cardo—began an observation club called the Nature Explorers on their own time after school—and each kept an observation journal. This is an excerpt from Mike's Nature Explorer journal:

April 19th
We went to Jorie's house to look at the birds. We saw a great blue heron, a snowy egret, and some ospreys. Then we went to Pussy's Pond. We went back to our secret places and discovered more of the spring. We went to the end of the spring but the rest of it is basically

only a puddle. But all of the Nature Explorers know there is still more to discover.

Isn't that our goal—to help our kids know how much more there is to discover? Lucille Clifton thinks that this wonder and amazement is how poetry first began. She says, "Poetry began when somebody walked off a savannah or out of a cave and looked up at the sky with wonder and said, 'Ahh.' That was the first poem. The urge towards 'Ah-h-h' is very human, it's in everybody. That urge is poetry."

OUTDOOR SKETCHING

In Alice Kamea's fourth grade at the Kamahameha School in Honolulu, Hawaii, all twenty-six of her students filed out of her room with pencils and notebooks in hand. The day was characteristically beautiful—late March, blue skies, 80 degrees, a light trade wind blowing. After braving the New York City winter I decided we would take advantage of the abundance of beauty here.

Alice, the kids, and I made a poetry huddle. I said to them, "Remember we're going to be scientists and poets today and the first thing to do is to find something out here in all this beauty that interests you. It could be a leaf, a flower, a grass blade, a tree, clouds, wind—whatever it is that you choose must interest and amaze you. When you find it, begin to see it by sketching—trace your pencil over what you're looking at like you're touching it. Don't worry if the drawing is good—that's not the point—it's really to see all those tiny details that we all miss because we pass by too quickly. And as you're drawing pay attention to what you're thinking. Sometimes when I draw I think to myself: What is this object like? Is it like anything else in the world? What does it remind me of? What surprises me about it? What's beautiful or amazing about it? Do I have any questions? And as you draw, write your thoughts down alongside your drawing. I usually draw a little, then write, then draw again, then write."

The kids then fanned out to different spots—some sat on the railing overlooking a clump of bushes, some sat on the sidewalk gazing intensely at dirt or grass, some stood and observed the big tree in front of us. I watched them as they walked around looking, sniffing, heads up to the sky, and down to the ground. I said to Alice, "Even if nobody writes a single poem today, to see kids appreciating the world like this is everything."

As they sketched, we walked around and quietly reminded them to be sure to write down whatever they were thinking as they drew (see Figure 5–3). This part, interrupting drawing to write, sometimes feels unnatural and takes getting used to.

After sketching for a while, we gathered in another poetry huddle—this time to share a little and prepare for the next step, which was to take some of their observations and create poems.

Figure 5–3   *Notebook page of tree*

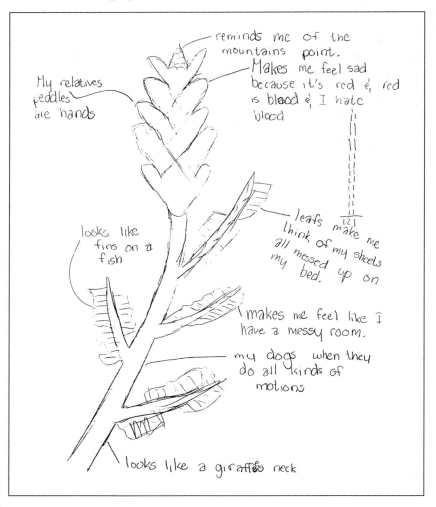

A few months later, the sixth graders at the Punahou School in Hawaii also went outside to draw and write. This time I called a poetry huddle in the middle of their sketching. When all the students had gathered I asked them to spin at least three similes (see Chapter 4) about what they were looking at, and write those beside their sketches. "For example," I said, "if I'm sketching that tree over there, I might say it looks like what? A piece of broccoli? A hand reaching up to the sky? Does anyone have any ideas?" One girl said enthusiastically, "It looks like a wig." "Yes! Just let your mind spin, and when you've spun at least three similes or metaphors underline those observations that feel particularly true or poetic, then try and create a poem from those observations." The fourth and sixth graders sketched and wrote wonderful poems that reflected their observations (see Figure 5–4).

OBSERVATION AND REVISION

Warren was a second grader in Fran Rosen's classroom. When I visited her classroom I asked the kids to search through their notebooks and underline lines of poems that had strong, vivid images; that resonated to them emotionally—or that they felt an attachment to; that gave them a feeling; or that just sounded like a poem. Warren underlined a part about his turtle (see Figure 5–5). He then read through and tried to put the excerpt into line-breaks by reading over his lines and listening for the pause—then making a slash mark where he heard the pause. In Figure 5–6, he is rearranging the lines in a variety of ways.

When I conferenced with him he was at this stage. "How are you doing, Warren?" "OK," he said. There was a long pause, which I let remain to see what else he would say. "I don't really like my poem."

I was a little surprised. I had read the poem briefly and it seemed like a good start. "Why?" I asked him.

"Because it doesn't really express what my turtle is like," he said.

"You know, Warren, why don't you go home tonight, be a scientist, and watch your turtle? You can take notes and see if you can add some of your observations to your poem." Warren agreed to do this, and I was curious what he would add to his poem. The next day during writing workshop I kneeled beside him. "How did it go last night?"

"Good," Warren said. "I think I finished my poem." He read his revised

Nature's Airport

It s branches stretch up just like arms
reaching for the sun,
Birds are always chirping there
as if they will never stop.
The branches sway in the wind like a monkey
doing a little crazy dance,
It s trunk is just like a condo,
a home for many creatures.

Once you take a look at the tree
and look at all of it s features,
You will see that it is busy
like Christmas shoppers rushing all about.
If you look left and right and all around
you will see birds flying in and out,
You will then agree
that it is nature's airport.

Figure 5–4   "Nature's Airport"

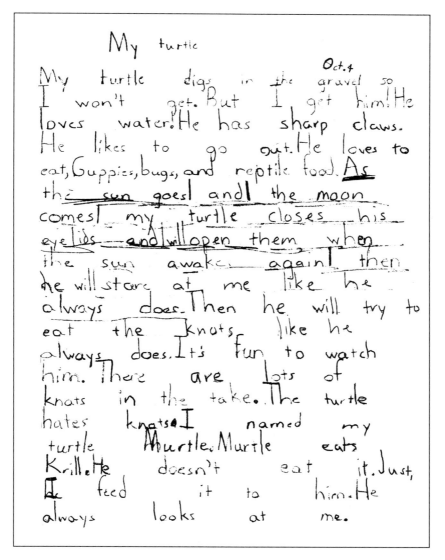

Figure 5–5   "My Turtle" in journal

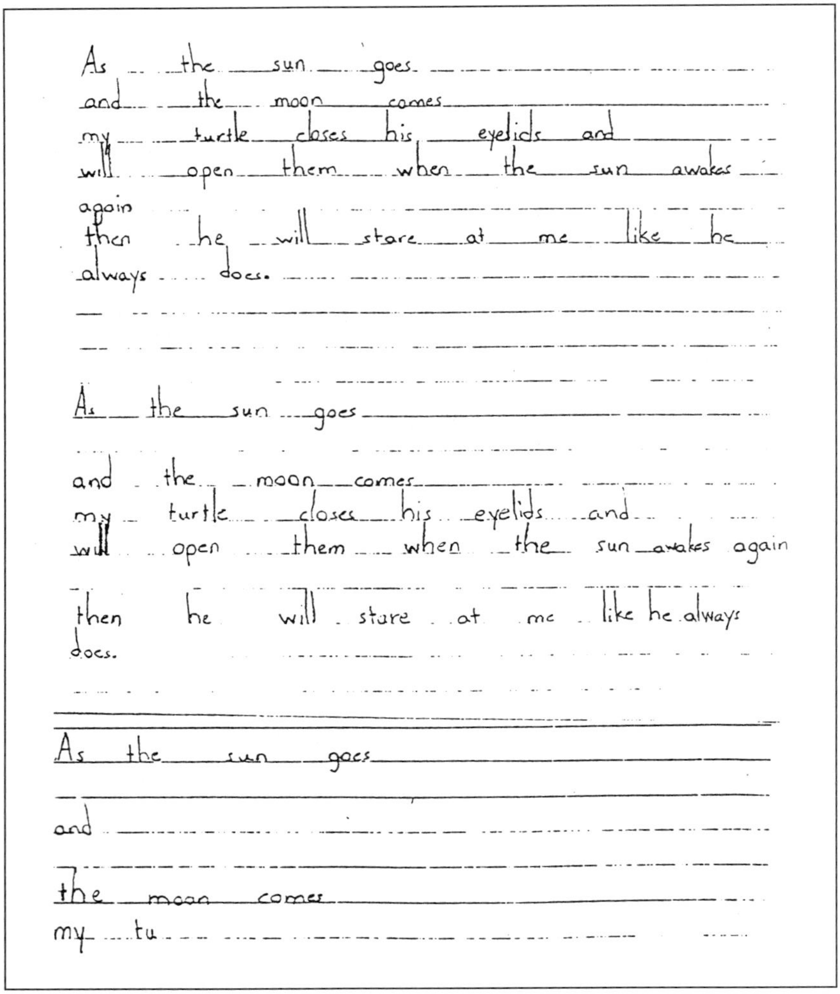

As the sun goes
and the moon comes
my turtle closes his eyelids and
will open them when the sun awakes
again
then he will stare at me like he
always does.

As the sun goes

and the moon comes
my turtle closes his eyelids and
will open them when the sun awakes again

then he will stare at me like he always
does.

As the sun goes

and

the moon comes
my tu

Figure 5–6   Turtle line arrangements

poem to me. I was amazed at how Warren's observations had helped him add accuracy to his poem (see Figure 5–7).

To see, and then to see again is part of what it means to write a poem. And this tool of reseeing is exactly what revision means—to literally see and resee. When I was a poetry student at Columbia University our teacher, Derek Walcott, advised that after every draft of a poem we sketch

My Turtle...
Sits there and does nothing.
His face out,
His neck in.
Legs are part
io,
Part out.
He opens his eyes
slowly.
Then stares.
Looks up,
Looks to the side,
Looks to the gravel
as green as grass
He reaches for the surface
but
he doesn't break it.
Quickly bobs his head
back in his shell.
Looking,
He sits there and does nothing.

Figure 5–7   "My Turtle" poem

the images that the words of the poem conjured in our minds to see what gaps we left out. To resee, whether it means actually observing something in the outside world or learning to observe our inner images, is an essential tool for poets.

Sharpening inner vision: Heart mapping

I gathered the third graders on the rug, as I usually do, and spoke of how poets write from their hearts about what we deeply care about. I told them that I write my poems from memories of my family, of growing up next to a creek in Virginia, and of the people I meet in my travels. Hands started to go up one by one, as kids were eager to tell their own important memory or something close to their hearts. After a few poets had shared I felt they understood where poems come from, so I sent them back to their tables to write their poems. As they hunched over their papers, writing, I walked around the room curious to read their poems. I glanced over Lacrisha's shoulder. Her poem went like this:

> Money, money, money is nice.
> Money, money, money is good.
> I like money.

I moved along and glanced at other poems, "I like to play Nintendo after school. It's really really fun." Most of the poems were quick sentences about what they liked but I didn't sense much heartfelt poetry. I knew I had to do something drastic.

The next day when I gathered the class together again I said, "Remember yesterday how we talked about that poets write from their hearts—what we really care about?" A few heads nodded. "Well, I was thinking last night that sometimes poets have to do some work first to know what's in their hearts, to know what they really care about, and what's really important to them. So today, we're going to do something very different—we're going to make maps of our hearts."

I heard a few whispers, "Maps of our hearts! What's that?"

"Today I'd like you to make a map of all the important things that are in your heart, all the things that really matter to you. You can put: people and places that you care about; moments and memories that have stayed with you; things you love to do, anything that has stayed in your heart because you care a lot about it. First, let's sit for a while, and I'd like you to think about what might go in the map of your heart."

After several minutes, one poet raised his hand and asked, "Can I put sports in my heart map?"

"If it's something that you really care about then it belongs in your map. Only you can decide what should be in your heart map."

They shared a few other ideas: grandmothers and grandfathers who had died; learning to sing; love felt for dogs, cats, and other pets; divorced parents; newly born brothers and sisters. They returned to their tables with colored pencils and white art paper to begin mapping their hearts.

By the time they returned to their seats, half the class had dragged their science books out of their desks and were tracing the small textbook heart, the size of a thumb, from their science books onto the white paper. I asked them to close their science books, and to draw the heart the way they wanted to express it: it could be a valentine heart; a scientific heart; they could draw two hearts—but I asked them to make sure the heart was large enough to fit their lives.

Once they began to draw and write, their hearts were amazing.

Lacrisha, who had inspired this project with her poem about money, divided her heart into segments of the people in her family. A crooked line ran down the left side of her heart dividing the words *brothers* and *sisters*. When I asked her what that meant, she said, "That's where my heart cracked—when my brothers and sisters and I were put into different foster homes."

Later, as they each had a chance to sit in the poet's chair to share their heart maps I learned what was truly important to these poets. I was amazed at how much more depth and feeling their heart maps contained compared to the poems they had written the previous day. This is often the case with beginning poets, especially if they haven't read a lot of poetry. Their stereotypes of what poetry should be like takes over any feeling they want to express. Creating heart maps helped them visualize and make concrete what they really cared about, and helped them sharpen their inner vision.

It's a poet's job to know the interior of his or her heart. This is one way of accessing these feelings. We carry this heart map around all the time but how many of us know what it really looks like and what's in it? Drawing a map of our hearts helps make order out of what often feels like chaos and reveals the meanings behind the confusing emotions. And these meanings shine like gems that have been long buried. All poems emanate from this inner terrain and the jewels that lie hidden there. Since that day in the third-grade classroom, I have asked many classes of all ages to map their hearts, and I am always surprised by what rises to the surface.

Here are some questions to help get your students started. These questions are only a guideline and are not meant to be "answered." Rather, they may help stimulate discussion before mapping. Begin by asking them what has stayed in their hearts:

What has really affected your heart?

What people have been important to you?

What are some experiences or central events that you will never forget?

What happy or sad memories do you have?

What secrets have you kept in your heart?

What small things or objects are important to you—a tree in your backyard, a trophy, a stuffed animal. . . ?

Here are some questions that students have explored in the past and used as techniques for drawing maps of their hearts:

Should some things be outside of the heart and some inside it?

Do you want to draw more than one heart—good and bad; happy and sad; secret and open—and include different things inside each heart?

What's at the center of your heart? What's outside around the edges?

Do different colors represent different emotions, events, relationships?

I'll always remember Shawntee, a student at a nurturing special education school in New York, who had a very difficult and complicated life: Shawntee's birth mother had died of a drug overdose when Shawntee was two years old. Shawntee's heart map was in the form of a letter to her mother, Dorothy (see Figure 5–8).

Shawntee hadn't been able to write about this experience before, but the heart mapping was concrete enough to enable her to feel the loss of her mother and express this loss within the drawing of her heart.

Gaspar, an eighth grader in a caring school in Arizona, wrote a poem

To. DOROThy

I Think about
My Mom. She made
he These Star cookies,
and whenever I Look
at The star in The
sky I Think about My
Mom in The sky With
The star,

from
Shawnte

Figure 5–8   Shawntee's poem to her mother

after mapping out his heart about how his heart is split in two: "My Latin Heart / My American Heart" (see Figure 5–9).

Keeping our hearts open is the work of poetry. Children are experts at it, as you can see in Figures 5–10 and 5–11. The point of heart mapping is not necessarily to write poems but to access the feelings, memories, and reflections that are the source of poetry: to sharpen our inner vision. Later, as an extension, I might ask students to select one part of their heart maps that they could explore in more detail, write a reflection from, and then write a poem.

FINDING YOUR INNER POET
In Cathy Grimes' second-grade class at the Worcester School in Connecticut we sat on the floor together in her warm, abundant classroom: plenty

My latin heart My American heart
My heart is falling
como un petalo de rosa en la tierra
My heart its going crazy
como un loco sin rumbo
My heart its scared
como un niño sin sus padres
My heart its lonely
Como una telaraña en mi cuarto
My heart its in love
Con la niña que nunca vendra
But I guess if I try my best
my corazon se curara.

Figure 5–9   "My Latin Heart / My American Heart"

of poetry books on the shelves, the students' writing, poems, and paintings hanging from the walls and ceilings. Each of her students had their notebooks and a pencil with them ready to take notes and share their poems. I began the discussion by writing three "inner poet" questions on a chart. These three questions were inspired by John Fox's book *Finding What You Didn't Lose:*

What does my inner poet look like?

What does my inner poet see?

When was my inner poet born?

At first her students seemed perplexed. They weren't quite sure what the questions meant. I gave an example of my own inner poet. "When I think of what my inner poet looks like it's a bird flying in the air and looking down

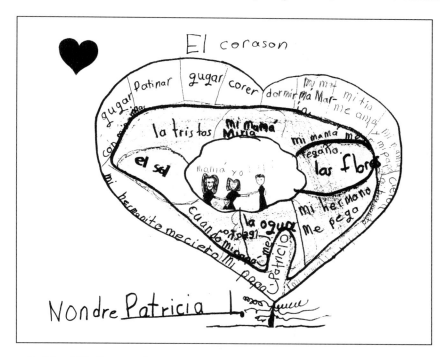

Figure 5–10   "El Corason"

on the world to get a new perspective. I can see the whole earth down below, and when I fly down toward the ground I can also see small things—worms and bugs in blades of grass. So my inner poet is like a bird—hungry for flying, soaring through the air, but also trying to notice the small things.

"Your inner poet is like a picture you get in your mind of how you feel when you're writing poetry: you could be an animal—anything in nature—a storm, a river. Think about who you are inside: How do you think of yourself? What is that person like inside who writes the poems you write? Is he or she different from the person you are in your everyday world? If you could give a face, a voice, a metaphor, or a simile of how you feel inside when you write your poems, what would it look like—a fish, a gliding swan, lightning?"

Kathryn spoke first. She said, "My inner poet is a wolf—it's all the fierce creatures in the world."

Cathy asked, "Kathryn, can you say more about this wolf?"

Karen, who was sitting next to Kathryn, said, "I'm the opposite. My inner poet is a soft, furry creature like a hamster or a rabbit. Soft and fuzzy."

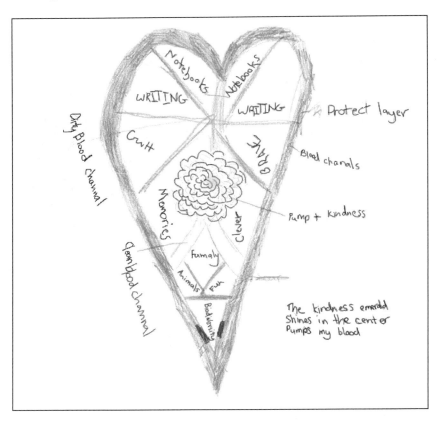

Figure 5–11   Heart with emerald center

Cathy said to me, "You know it's true of their poetry too. Kathryn's poetry is fierce—much more like a wolf—and Karen's is soft and more like a rabbit."

Our discussion continued as other students began to express what their inner poets looked like. Then we asked them to freewrite in their notebooks about their inner poets using the three questions on the chart as a guide.

As I walked around the room talking with students, I was amazed at the insights they had into themselves, their personalities, and their inner poets. Kathyrn wrote this poem, "Wolf You Are My Brother."

> Wolf you are my brother
> my inner poet, as well.

You prowl around
watching . . . watching
the moon.

You do give me a free
feeling.
I love your cry when you present it
to the moon.

Wolf you are my brother
my inner poet as well.

Brian wrote "Inner Poet":

My inner poet is a Bird. Have you
ever seen a bird flying into a window
and then falling to the ground?
That's what I've felt in the past
when I'm writing. But now I'm a bird
that soars over the house.
Sometimes I feel like a lion that is
always hungry for poems.

Caitlin described her inner poet as a dog:

My Dog Poet
My inner poet
is my dog
running free
on my paper
wagging its tail
sometimes it
is on a leash
when it is
on a leash
I am sick—
held away from
my poetry until I
am better.
She won't ever be bad.
Never has and never will.

I can tell she will
never be bad to me
for the
whole life of me.
The dog and me both have love,
love for each other
with that love
the dog will always be there
waiting for poetry.

And Summer wrote "About Me":

My inner poet is like a duck
ducking its head underwater looking for poetry.

My inner poet thinks
I can write about worms, fish, rainbows, friends,
anything.
I can even write about food.

My inner poet is a poem digester.

A cat scratching itself thinking poetry.
My Cat inner poet loves to think and talk.

A turtle walking slowly,
day dreaming poetry.
Sometimes it takes a long time writing poetry,
that's when I use my Turtle inner poet.

I think all the people in the world have an
inner reader,
inner poet,
inner player, and
inner mathematician.

As I travel,
my Cat and my Turtle will travel.

How we see ourselves inside determines how and why we write, and
what poems we choose to read and cherish. It's the work of knowing ourselves from the inside—rather than from the outside—sharpening our inner vision that lies at the heart of writing poetry.

Epilogue
YOURSELF AS THE KEY

Several years ago I took a trip back to Oldfields—to my grandparents' summer home. This was after my ninety-nine-year-old grandmother had died and I wanted to see what I could see and remember. As I drove down the driveway, memories came rushing back to me—the ghost of me as a girl walking down to get the mail, my grandfather in his garden tending the roses.

It was like pentimento—the process of painting, for example, a portrait of a woman on the canvas, then scraping it out and repainting it, layering more paint on top of the first layer. *Pentimento* is the term used to describe what happens to the canvas hundreds of years later, when the ghost of the first image begins to show through under the current image.

I walked out in the woods to see if I could find the mound of stones where I dug thirty years before. I walked and walked; all I found were scattered rocks, not anything like I remembered. It occurred to me that perhaps all this mystery surrounding Oldfields had been in my imagination, fueled by my grandfather's words; it was my way of searching for the mysteries of life. I asked myself, Is this really all that I saw when I was a child? Or had time scattered the rocks and made them smaller?

I stared a long time, trying to re-create that childhood memory of spending the afternoon digging through layers of rock and dirt. And as I stood there, I realized that this is precisely what poetry is about: from a glimpse, a memory, an image, we re-create our worlds, we build mounds from scattered rocks, we sift through our lives and find poems.

This recurring image of Oldfields and of digging through the layers to get to the truth of something has guided my work as a poet as well as a teacher of poetry for almost twenty years now.

Poetry has the power to change us, by helping us sift through the layers of our lives in search of our own truths and our own poems. The students we teach sometimes have an easier time than adults knowing and expressing these often hidden layers of feelings and experiences. Matthew Fox wrote:

> The Celtic peoples . . . insisted that *only the poets could be teachers.* Why? I think it is because knowledge that is not passed through the heart is dangerous.

The work of teaching poetry is the work of letting knowledge pass through our hearts: sharpening our own outer and inner visions; writing and reading poetry; and helping to awaken poetry in ourselves and in all of our students. The more we let ourselves feel poetry, the easier it is to teach it. All of us are hungry to express our true selves, to be reunited with our hearts, and this is the real work of teaching and exploring poetry. As Eve Merriam describes in her poem "Poem As a Door":

> If you expect it to be bolted,
> it will be.
>
> There is only one opening:
> yourself as the key.

Appendix A

Guidelines for Revising Your Own Poem, Peer Conferring, and Response Groups

1. Read the poem out loud.
2. Ask someone else to read your poem back to you—it helps to hear your poem read in a different voice so you can listen to the poem more objectively.
3. As you listen to your poem ask yourself some of these questions:

Are there any words or lines that sound awkward, that clink on the page?

What words or lines sound strong, pleasing, "poetic," or memorable?

Are there any words or lines that sound stale or clichéd?

Does the poem make you feel anything?

Which words, lines, or images move you the most?

Does the poem feel emotionally true?

Are there any words or images that feel untrue?

Is the poem clear or does it feel confused?

Can you see the images in the poem? Are they clear, powerful, concrete, and vivid?

As you're listening do you see any other images in your mind that you could add?

Is the poem abstract in any places—does this strengthen or weaken the poem?

Does the poem "explain"—rather than "show"?

Does the "energy" leak out of the poem? Does your mind begin to wander?

What words, images, rhythms, or thoughts catch you by surprise—give you that ahhh! feeling?

Appendix B
Poets as Teachers

Poets have a crowd of invisible teachers in our hearts and heads giving us advice and tips on how to write our poems. We need to people our classrooms with as many "teachers" as we can. My goal is to help students find their poetry mentors, so instead of only one teacher in the room there are many. The following is a list of some poets who have been my teachers, and a list of what they can teach our students. For a complete listing of books, see Appendix D and References.

Writing with Metaphor and Simile, Saying Things in a New Way, Finding Poetry in the Ordinary:

Valerie Worth, *all the small poems and fourteen more*

Pablo Neruda, *Odes to Common Things*

Naomi Shihab Nye, *Words Under the Words*

Ralph Fletcher, *Ordinary Things*

Debra Chandra, *Rich Lizard and Other Poems*

Interesting Rhyme:

Eve Merriam, *The Singing Green*

Langston Hughes, *The Dreamkeeper and Other Poems*

Eloise Greenfield, *Honey, I Love*

Robert Frost, *Complete Poems of Robert Frost*

Pattern and Repetition:

Eloise Greenfield, *Honey, I Love*

Observation:

Valerie Worth, *all the small poems and fourteen more*

Debra Chandra, *Rich Lizard and Other Poems*

Mary Oliver, *White Pine: Poems and Prose Poems*

Autobiographical/Writing Personal Truths:

Lee Bennett Hopkins, *Been to Yesterdays*

Donald Graves, *Baseball, Snakes, and Summer Squash*

Myra Cohn Livingston, *There Was a Place and Other Poems*

Sharon Olds, *The Wellspring*

Liz Rosenberg, ed., *The Invisible Ladder: An Anthology of Contemporary American Poems for Young Readers*

Word Play:

Eve Merriam, *The Singing Green*

Barbara Juston Esbensen, *Words with Wrinkled Knees*

Line-Breaks:

Arnold Adoff, *Sports Pages* and *Street Music: City Poems*

William Carlos Williams, *Collected Poems 1909–1939*

Image:

Lilian Moore, *I Thought I Heard the City Sing*

Paul Janeczko, ed., *Pocket Poems*

Gary Soto, *A Fire in My Hands*

Appendix C
Anthology of Student Poetry

Great Grandpa
Andrea Metcalf, Grade 5

Part of life shattered
like a fallen icicle.
My grandpa died.
An unfamiliar pain came over me
like a bowling ball hitting ten pins.
I cried for days,
but my heart still has love,
happiness,
and a smell I'll never forget,
cinnamon.
I'll remember his soft hands,
cheeks,
and hair as white as cotton.
Grandpa, why did you
have to die?
I loved you then;
I'll love you always.

The Basketball

Alexander W. Marcus, Grade 4

An orange sphere,
Hard in your hands,
With tiny bumps all over,
As if it has the chicken pox,
It soars like an eagle in the sky,
Curving up and diving down into its nest.

The Sun's Light

James Terdiman, Grade 4

The sun's brightness gets brighter each hour
Just like me
The sun gets up in the morning
Just like me
The sun goes to sleep on its soft cushion
Just like I sleep in my warm bed
The difference between the sun and me is that . . .
It just sits in one place,
While I play in its shine

Lemon

Carolyn Cohen, Grade 4

Watch the football shaped moon,
Roll around like a great round barrel
Look closely at its tiny sparkles,
Its bright color.
Close to my face
With its sweet smell,
I feel as if my grandmother is holding me
With her tender hands.

The World

Nicole Ariyoshi, Grade 1

The world is like a precious egg
a very smooth soft egg
and is just about to crack.

When armies go on every inch
the egg cracks.
Turn it around!

Thinking
Deborah Cinanni, Grade 4

Are you curious?
Well are you?
Take your time
and ask yourself
again—
Are you curious?

Sea Song (On a clear northwest breezy day)
Tony Hack, Grade 4

Sea and brightness,
Sea and the glittering white caps of the waves,
Sea and the song of all tides.
Rising and falling
Playful souls of the ocean,
Beat on me like sun rays on the earth.

How to Make a Poem
Danielle Pioggia, Grade 3

Close your eyes.
Don't peek.
Close them tight,
tight so it's
dark, dark
till you see something
in sight.

Close your eyes
don't peek.
Try
and see a poem.

Poetry Hides

Marissa Foran, Grade 1

Poetry hides
in a bag of
chips because
it crunches
like leaves in the fall.

Scissors

Nicholas Thompson, Grade 5

Scissors—
Cutting—
Hair, Cardboard, Paper.

Scissors—
Useful—
Tool, Sharp, Big, Small.

Scissors—
Double Cutting Edge—
Hearts, Paper Dolls, Shapes.

Space

Charlie Allen, Grade 6

As I look through the telescope
And see the stars
The comets
The asteroids
All acting out the never ending play
The Romeos
The Juliets
So close but yet so far
The births
The deaths
Of the never ending play
As we act out our parts
And we'll never be replaced
Because no role is different
And no role is the same.

Stars Are Born

Jeff Frumess, Grade 5

Every time you see a star,
An angel gets its wings.
Every time a baby is born,
A bird flies for the first time.
Every time someone dies,
A leaf falls to the ground.
Every time a man works hard,
A bumble bee gets to rest.
Every time an angel's wing breaks,
A star dies.

When Is Tomorrow?

Julia Salem, Grade 1
(Dedicated to her mom)

When is tomorrow?
When the flowers bloom.
Those flowers are like
your rosy cheeks.
When is tomorrow?
When we go to crystal land?
(crystal land is like your sparkly eyes).
When is tomorrow? What is it?
It's when we see
god in a meadow
with the secret valley
of nature.
This is all you.
Tomorrow is you.

The Wind, the Wind

Breahna Arnold, Grade 2

The wind, the wind
is singing a sweet song.
The trees, the trees
are dancing through the sky.
The clouds, the clouds

are whispering.
The bees, the bees
are buzzing in my ear.
The wind, the wind.
The trees, the trees.
The clouds, the clouds.
The bees, the bees.
A new story has been told.

1775 Mulford Farm
Lily Henderson, Grade 6

The sounds of the fife come into my ears
Playing all kinds of music.
A man carves wooden birds,
Women show their quilts.
And somewhere a chicken with a wrung neck
Is cooking in a pot.
The militia fires its guns
And America's history begins.
Here I am standing in the middle of 200 years
Before I was born.

The Happy Whale
Garrett Collier, Grade 1

If I were a whale
I would watch the sky
hum to the seagulls,
watch the fish games,
then curiously
want to see
what color my tongue is.

Wet Leaves
Scott Thelander, Grade 2

after
the gloomy
clouds
go away

from
the rain forest
water
dingles off
the little
wet leaves

Untitled
Brody, Kindergarten

The fish swims
in the streams
around
the rocks to
destiny

Scary Tale
David Eichhorn, Grade 4

Scary
Scary
Scary
Scary
Scary
Scary
Scary
Scary
Scary
Scary
Tale

Is

Very
Very
Very
Very
Very
Very
Dull

Onions
Marci Kang, Grade 1

Onions make you
cry with all your might.
You try not to
but the onion always wins.

Untitled
Jessica, Kindergarten

I saw a shooting star
and I made a wish
that my dad
would never
have to wear glasses.

My Jewelry Box
Moe Hyuga, Grade 4

Covered with flowers
That shine all day.

As bright
As the stars in night.

Blue
Like the sky up above.

Women/girls wear what's inside,
They feel comfortable with their touch.

My Baseball
Rebecca Mollie Goldberg, Grade 4

Smooth and round,
like a star in the sky,
sewn in red with
bloody lines.
Hard like a gray diamond,
floating, flying
swiftly through the air,
toward a giant white bird,
soaring to its leather brown mom.

A great white bird,
as it lands on its great
white tomb.

The Countdown
Jed Serby, Grade 5

Two, Two Yah-hoo
One, One "Have Fun"
Zero, Zero It's My Hero
Bbbzzzz
Out, Out to your home
Then brush your hair with a comb!
You will have a good
Vacation!
Maybe in another
Nation!
For 2 months you might be
Looking at a hollow tree
In the Darkness and the Damp.
"Goodbye students,
Goodbye!"
The teacher yells
As they run out
The door!
The hall is quiet once more.

Playmates
Sarah Webb, Grade 1

Playmates are the best friends ever.
They make me feel
like more than I am.

Untitled
Betsy Welsh and Julianne Befler, Grade 3
(Poem for two voices)

The wind is blowing

       swiiiish
       The trees are swaying

In the water the rocks
look like mountains

The water makes ripples

sphagnum covers the
trees

The forest sticks and
stones form a path
The lake is calm

Soon there's a
meadow
The weeds are
tall and damp

In the water the rocks
look like mountains

that look like fish
sphagnum covers the
trees
The trees are naked
The forest sticks and
stones form a path

and only one fish
dares to jump
Soon there's a
meadow

now everyone
knows winter is
coming.

Stuffed Animals in My Bed
Caitlin, Grade 5

Like water overflowing a pool
Or shells filling the ocean
They are my blankets, full of life
Lined up on the bed spread.
They are my army, navy and marines
Protecting me from all bad dreams
Stuffed with clouds covered with the thick sky
They are the last things I see at night
And the first in the morning

The Angels' Sky
Shawn Allen, Grade 1

The sky is an angel's pools.
God is their lifeguard.
They have their diving board,
they jump off a plane that flies by.
The sky is an angel's pool.

Untitled

Ryan Burns, Grade 1

Poetry hides
in my heart. . . .

How Do You Write a Poem?

Brent Tatsuno and Alvin Kamm, Grade 6
(Poem for two voices)

How do you write a poem?

    You look in your heart.

What are your feelings?

    Your surroundings?

Your imaginings?
Your wonderings?
    Your wonderings?
What do you see?

    Seek the image.
The image.
    The image.
An empty room.
    A pepper plant.
An alley cat.
    A rocking chair.
How do you write a poem?

    Weave in surprises.

Life is one long lei.

    And each person is a different flower.

The ocean.

    And shore.
In constant battle.
    In constant battle.
How do you write a poem?

    Unusual words.

Let the rain
Kiss you.
    Kiss you.
Line breaks.

    Ordinary to poetic.

Repetition.

    Repetition.

A song of your heart.
That's how you write a poem!
    That's how you write a poem!

Appendix D
A Few Good Poetry Books

Adoff, Arnold. 1995. *Street Music: City Poems.* New York: Harper-Collins.

———. 1981. *Outside Inside: Poems.* New York: Harcourt Brace & Co.

Brenner, Barbara, ed. 1994. *The Earth Is Painted Green: A Garden of Poems About Our Planet.* New York: Scholastic.

Bryan, Ashley. 1997. *ABC of African American Poetry.* New York: Atheneum.

Carlson, Lori M. 1994. *Cool Salsa: Bilingual Poems on Growing Up Latino in the United States.* New York: Henry Holt.

Chandra, Deborah. 1993. *Rich Lizard and Other Poems.* New York: Farrar, Straus & Giroux.

Esbensen, Barbara. 1996. *Echoes for the Eye: Poems to Celebrate Patterns in Nature.* New York: HarperCollins.

———. 1995. *Dance with Me.* New York: HarperCollins.

Fletcher, Ralph. 1997. *Ordinary Things: Poems from a Walk in Early Spring.* New York: Atheneum.

———. 1997. *Room Enough for Love: The Complete Poems from* I Am Wings *and* Buried Alive. New York: Aladdin Paperbacks.

Lynne, Sandford, ed. 1996. *Ten-Second Rain Showers: Poems by Young People.* New York: Simon & Schuster.

Moon, Pat. 1996. *Earth Lines: Poems for the Green Age.* New York: Greenwillow.

Moore, Lilian. 1997. *Poems Have Roots: New Poems by Lilian Moore.* New York: Atheneum.

Mora, Pat. 1996. *Confetti: Poems for Children.* New York: Lee and Low Books.

Myers, Walter Dean. 1993. *Brown Angels: An Album of Pictures and Verse.* New York: HarperCollins.

Nye, Naomi Shihab. 1995. *The Tree Is Older Than You Are: A Bilingual Gathering of Poems & Stories from Mexico with Paintings by Mexican Artists.* New York: Simon & Schuster.

————. 1995. *Words Under the Words.* Portland, OR: The Eighth Mountain Press.

————, ed. 1992. *This Same Sky: A Collection of Poems from Around the World.* New York: Four Winds Press.

Nye, Naomi Shihab, and Paul Janeczko, eds. 1996. *I Feel A Little Jumpy Around You: A Book of Her Poems & His Poems Collected in Pairs.* New York: Simon & Schuster.

Oliver, Mary. 1994. *White Pine: Poems and Prose Poems.* New York: Harcourt Brace & Company.

Soto, Gary. 1995. *Canto Familiar.* New York: Harcourt Brace & Company.

————. 1990. *A Fire in My Hands.* New York: Scholastic.

Stevenson, James. 1995. *Sweet Corn: Poems.* New York: Greenwillow.

Wong, Janet S. 1996. *A Suitcase of Seaweed and Other Poems.* New York: Simon & Schuster.

Wood, Nancy. 1993. *Spirit Walker.* New York: Doubleday.

References

Adoff, Arnold. 1979. *Eats.* New York: Lothrop, Lee & Shepard Books.

Bly, Robert, ed. 1986. *The Winged Life: The Poetic Voice of Henry David Thoreau.* New York: HarperCollins.

Chandra, Deborah. 1990. *Balloons.* New York: Farrar, Straus & Giroux.

Dacey, Philip. 1977. *How I Escaped from the Labyrinth and Other Poems.* Pittsburgh, PA: Carnegie-Mellon University Press.

Ernst, Karen. 1993. *Picturing Learning.* Portsmouth, NH: Heinemann.

Esbenson, Barbara. 1987. *Words with Wrinkled Knees.* New York: Harper-Collins.

Espada, Martin, ed. 1994. *Poetry Like Bread: Poets of the Political Imagination.* Willimantic, CT: Curbstone Press.

Fletcher, Ralph. 1997. *Twilight Comes Twice.* Boston: Houghton Mifflin Company.

Fox, John. 1995. *Finding What You Didn't Lose: Expressing Your Truth and Creativity Through Poem-Making.* New York: Tarcher/Putnum.

Fox, Matthew. 1995. *The Reinvention of Work: A New Vision of Livelihood for Our Time.* New York: HarperCollins.

Franck, Frederick. 1993. *Zen Seeing, Zen Drawing: Meditation in Action.* New York: Bantam Books.

Frost, Robert. 1964. *Complete Poems of Robert Frost.* New York: Holt, Rinehart, and Winston.

George, Jean Craighead. 1984. *One Day in the Alpine Tundra.* New York: Thomas Y. Crowell.

Graves, Donald. 1996. *Baseball, Snakes, and Summer Squash: Poems of Childhood.* Honesdale, PA: Boyds Mills Press.

Greenfield, Eloise. 1978. *Honey, I Love.* New York: HarperCollins.

Heard, Georgia. 1997. *Creatures of Earth, Sea, and Sky.* Honesdale, PA: Boyds Mills Press.

Hopkins, Lee Bennett, ed. 1995. *Good Times, Good Books.* New York: HarperCollins.

———. 1987. *Click, Rumble, Roar: Poems About Machines.* New York: Thomas Y. Crowell.

Hughes, Langston. 1994. *The Dreamkeeper and Other Poems.* New York: Alfred A. Knopf.

———. 1974. *Selected Poems of Langston Hughes.* New York: Random House.

Hugo, Richard. 1992. *The Triggering Town: Lectures and Essays on Poetry and Writing.* New York: Norton.

Janeczko, Paul, ed. 1990. *The Place My Words Are Looking For.* New York: Bradbury Press.

———, ed. 1985. *Pocket Poems.* New York: Bradbury Press.

Kunitz, Stanley. 1985. *Next-to-Last Things: New Poems and Essays.* New York: The Atlantic Monthly Press.

———. 1979. *The Poems of Stanley Kunitz: 1928–1978.* Boston: Little, Brown.

Little, Jean. 1986. *Hey World, Here I Am.* New York: HarperCollins.

Merriam, Eve. 1992. *The Singing Green.* New York: William Morrow.

———. 1976. *Rainbow Writing.* New York: Atheneum.

Merwin, W. S. 1973. *Writing to an Unfinished Accompaniment.* New York: Atheneum.

Milosz, Czeslaw. 1978. *Bells in Winter.* Translated by author and Lillian Vallee. New York: The Ecco Press.

Moore, Lilian. 1969. *I Thought I Heard the City Sing.* New York: Atheneum.

———. 1967. *I Feel the Same Way.* New York: Atheneum.

Moyers, Bill, ed. 1995. *The Language of Life: A Festival of Poets.* New York: Doubleday.

Nash, Ogden. 1940. *The Face Is Familiar.* New York: Little, Brown.

Neruda, Pablo. 1994. *Odes to Common Things.* New York: Little, Brown.

Nye, Naomi Shihab. 1994. *Red Suitcase.* New York: BOA Editions.

Olds, Sharon. 1996. *The Wellspring.* New York: Knopf.

Oliver, Mary. 1995. *Blue Pastures.* Orlando, FL: Harcourt Brace & Company.

Peacock, Molly, Elise Paschen, and Neil Neches, eds. 1996. *Poetry in Motion: 100 Poems from the Subways and Buses.* New York: W. W. Norton.

Peterson, Ralph. 1992. *Life in a Crowded Place.* Portsmouth, NH: Heinemann.

Rosenberg, Liz, ed. 1996. *The Invisible Ladder: An Anthology of Contemporary American Poems for Young Readers.* New York: Henry Holt.

Ruben, Robert Alden, ed. 1993. *Poetry Out Loud.* New York: Workman Publishing.

Rylant, Cynthia. 1986. *Night in the Country.* New York: Bradbury Press.

Sandburg, Carl. Sel. by Lee Bennett Hopkins. 1982. *Rainbows Are Made.* Orlando, FL: Harcourt Brace and Company.

Simic, Charles. 1974. *Return to a Place Lit by a Glass of Milk.* New York: Georges Braziller.

Ward, Leila. 1978. *I am eyes: ni macho.* New York: Greenwillow Books.

Williams, William Carlos. 1938. *Collected Poems 1909–1939, Vol.1.* New York: New Directions.

Worth, Valerie. 1994. *all the small poems and fourteen more.* New York: Farrar, Straus & Giroux.

Yolen, Jane. 1987. *Owl Moon.* New York: Philomel Books.